S0-BTD-811

WITHDRAWN

New York's
First Theatrical Center
The Rialto at Union Square

Theater and Dramatic Studies, No. 26

Oscar G. Brockett, Series Editor
Leslie Waggener Professor of Fine Arts
and Professor of Drama
The University of Texas at Austin

Bernard Beckerman, Series Editor, 1980-1983
Brander Matthews Professor of Dramatic Literature
Columbia University in the City of New York

Other Titles in This Series

New York's First Theatrical Center
The Rialto at Union Square

by
John W. Frick

Assistant Professor of Communication Arts
University of Wisconsin Center—Fond du Lac
Fond du Lac, Wisconsin

UMI RESEARCH PRESS
Ann Arbor, Michigan

Copyright © 1985, 1983
John W. Frick
All rights reserved

Produced and distributed by
UMI Research Press
an imprint of
University Microfilms International
A Xerox Information Resources Company
Ann Arbor, Michigan 48106

Library of Congress Cataloging in Publication Data

Frick, John W.
  New York's first theatrical center.

  (Theater and dramatic studies ; no. 26)
  "A revision of the author's doctoral thesis, New York University,
1983"—T.p. verso.
  Bibliography: p.
  1. Theater—New York (N.Y.)—History—19th century.
2. New York (N.Y.)—Popular culture—History—19th century.
3. New York (N.Y.)—Theaters. 4. New York (N.Y.)—   PN
Amusements. I. Title. II. Series. III. Title: Union   1256
Square.   F68
                                                             1985
PN2256.F68   1984   792'.09747'1   84-16255
ISBN 0-8357-1612-0 (alk. paper)

Contents

List of Figures

Acknowledgments

I wish to thank the many people who aided me in the research and writing of this study. My first thanks are extended to Professor Brooks McNamara, Department of Performance Studies, New York University, whose guidance, encouragement, and sage and timely advice shaped the final product, and to Dr. Mary Henderson, whose book *The City and the Theatre* and whose class at New York University planted the seeds from which this study grew.

For their painstaking efforts in locating and providing research materials, I am indebted to the following: Wendy Warnken of the Theatre Collection and Jennifer Bright of the Print Archives at the Museum of the City of New York; Dorothy Swerdlove and the staff of the Billy Rose Theatre Collection, New York Public Library; Louis Rachow at The Players; Jeanne Newlin, Martha Mahard, and the staff at the Harvard Theatre Collection; Mary Ann Jensen at the Princeton Theatre Collection; Katherine Richards and the staff of the Research Library, New York Historical Society; Wendy Shadwell of the Prints Division, New York Historical Society; Gunther Pohl, Barbara Hillman, and Frank Bradley of the Local History and Genealogy Division, New York Public Library; Mary Corliss of the Film Stills Archives at the Museum of Modern Art; Charling Fagan at the Avery Library; Abbott Van Nostrand at Samuel French, Inc.; the staffs of the Art and Architecture, Maps, Special Collections, and Newspaper Divisions of the New York Public Library; the staff of the Records Division, New York City Department of Finance; the staff of the Engineering Society Library; and the reference staff of The Berkshire Athenaeum.

My special thanks to Stephen Burge Johnson and Stephen Vallillo, who listened many times to my ideas and also unearthed valuable information on my subject while conducting their own research; to Maryann Chach for details no one else could furnish; to Jack Frick, who rendered the maps; and to Marsha Van Benschoten Frick, whose patience, moral support, and assistance enabled me to finish this study.

1

Emergence of a Theatrical Center

In the years between 1870 and 1900, an actor seeking employment, lodging, or a congenial meal with a colleague gravitated not to Times Square, as he might today, but to the junction of Broadway, the Bowery, and 14th St.—to Union Square. While curiosity seekers strolled up and down 14th St. looking for celebrities, managers of road companies patrolled the east and south sides of the square, an area known to actors as the "slave market." On the benches in this part of the square, managers conducted open-air negotiations with prospective members of next year's company. When bargaining broke down, differences often could be resolved at one of the small round tables in the nearby Morton House bar, in the comfortable atmosphere of the restaurant in the Hotel Hungaria, or over a five-course dinner at the Union Square Hotel dining room. Throughout the area, vendors peddled their wares from pushcarts and from the small shops that lined the square and the neighboring streets. All were drawn to the vicinity for the same reason: Union Square was the Rialto, the center of New York's first modern theatre district (fig. 1).

At its inception in 1870, "New York's first major theatrical district actually began below Union Square with the few holdovers from [the past, including] Niblo's Garden, the Theatre Comique, the Olympic, Lina Edward's Theatre . . . and the Globe," and extended to Madison Square, the location of the Fifth Avenue Theatre, then occupied by Augustin Daly and his company.[1] The district, at the time, contained such famous houses as Booth's Theatre, Koster and Bial's Music Hall, and Pike's Opera House, all on 23rd St., and the New Park Theatre on Broadway at 22nd St. Within the larger theatre district, the Rialto or epicenter of theatrical activity occupied a relatively small amount of land, extending from 2nd Ave. on the east to 7th Ave. on the west, and from 9th St. on the south to 19th St. on the north.

Paradoxically, during Union Square's Rialto period (1870-1900), a relatively small proportion of the city's major theatres (The Academy of Music, Wallack's, the Union Square Theatre, the Fourteenth Street Theatre) were actually within the boundaries of the Rialto; nevertheless, Union Square was recognized by both theatre professionals and the general public as the hub of theatrical activity because so many of the enterprises that supported the theatre were located there. The blocks

Figure 1.   Union Square in Midsummer, 1882. A chromo-lithograph showing many of the theatrical enterprises located on the square. The scene is surrounded by pictures of stars of the New York Stage.
(Courtesy of the Theatre Collection, Museum of the City of New York)

surrounding the square were monopolized by the offices of theatrical agents; by hotels, bars, and restaurants that catered to actors and theatre-goers alike; by costume houses, scenery shops, manufacturers of stage properties, theatrical printers, stage photographers, trade newspapers, and shops that sold the latest foreign and domestic scripts.

At the beginning of the nineteenth century, such a theatre district did not exist and, in fact, could not have existed. The emergence of a specialized district for entertainment resulted from the convergence of several trends, nonexistent in 1800, but readily apparent at mid-century—the growth of a mass audience, an increasing desire for diversity in amusement, the creation of businesses designed to provide goods and services for the theatre, and the evolution of specialized commercial districts of all sorts in the city.

During the 1820s, a popular theatre—unsophisticated, nationalistic, anti-intellectual, and highly visual—began to emerge as the laborer and the recent transplant from the farm and small town began to attend plays in larger numbers. Increasingly, the common man was drawn to the theatre by dramatic elements that catered directly to his tastes—melodramas with their simple plots, comprehensible morals, clearly defined characters, and gripping climactic scenes where good invariably triumphed over evil; spectacular scenic effects; the portrayal of the "rustic, proud, independent, morally strong, brave, and nationalistic" stage Yankee by James Hackett, George H. Hill, Dan Marble, and others; and, the appearance of Edwin Forrest, the first major American-born star and idol of the working man.[2]

By the early 1830s popular theatres were a fait accompli, co-existing with the theatres usually patronized by the wealthy and educated. New, larger houses provided the fare demanded by the common man at prices scaled to his pocketbook (75, 50, and 37½ cents). Thus, the Park and Burton's remained bastions of the genteel theatre-goer, but the Bowery, the National, and the Chatham became recognized by the working classes as their own special places of entertainment. While New York's first families were treated to the talents of Charles Kemple and his daughter, Fanny, at the Park during the 1832-33 season, the masses flocked to the Bowery to witness *Mazeppa* with its spectacular climactic scene in which the hero is strapped to the back of a "wild charger."

For the next 20 years, there was no attempt to establish theatres in a central location. "Theatre managers and builders ranged throughout the city in search of sites which would attract the greatest following . . . [and] playhouses were located in the old and new sections and in all directions."[3] There was a small cluster of theatres at Park Row, and a handful of theatres on Broadway from City Hall to just south of Houston St. The Bowery Theatre and Bowery Amphitheatre were located on the lower Bowery just north of Bayard St., while Vauxhall Gardens was situated farther up the same thoroughfare near the present E. 4th St. Roughly half a dozen theatres were scattered in the regions west of Broadway, with the Richmond Hill Theatre, on Varick St. near Vandam, far to the north and west of New York's center of activity, City Hall.

Between 1840 and 1870, both the city and the theatre experienced a boom period of unprecedented proportions. During this period, the city shed the remaining vestiges of its colonial past and became a crowded and bustling metropolis. It had survived a depression between 1837 and 1843 and had experienced 25 years of uninterrupted expansion. Swelled by large-scale immigrations from Ireland and Germany, the population increased by 250 percent and the city's population centers shifted dramatically.[4] By 1870, more than one-half of New York's inhabitants lived north of 14th St., which had been the northern limit of the city in 1845, and the city's geographic center had moved from City Hall to Union Square.

During the quarter of a century between 1845 and 1870, there was a similar explosion in the amusement business, which permanently altered the nature of entertainment in this country. With a growing proportion of the population in the industrialized urban centers composed of immigrants and migrants from America's rural areas, "new means of amusement had to be found to replace those from which increasingly large numbers of persons were cut off by the very circumstance of city life."[5] In his quest for escape from the drudgery of his daily activities and his desire to replace the forms of recreation he had sacrificed when he moved to the city, the working man sought refuge in entertainments of all sorts and increasingly demanded greater diversity in his amusements.

Not surprisingly, many popular entertainment forms developed during this era. The black-face minstrel show, emerging from the Afro-American songs and dances performed by "Jim Crow" Rice and other Ethiopian delineators in the 1830s, literally swept the nation during the forties, rivaling the legitimate stage in popularity. Variety, the raunchy precursor of vaudeville, composed of a loosely-knit series of songs, dances, novelty acts, sketches, and flagrantly "blue" jokes, was presented for all-male audiences throughout the city in museums, saloons, and concert halls, as well as in a handful of specialized variety houses. Likewise, circuses and panoramas (large pictorial representations of landscapes or other scenes, painted on canvas) grew in popularity and proliferated in New York, utilizing any space large enough to accommodate them. Lectures, first introduced in the 1820s, reached a new height of popularity in the 1840s as "the general public [rushed] to the lecture as they might formerly have done to a play."[6] The diversity that blossomed during the forties would later become part of the iconography of the modern entertainment center, which offered amusements for all tastes, from grand opera to tawdry variety.

It was one of these new popular forms, the minstrel show, that provided the impetus for the clustering of theatres along Broadway. In the fifties and sixties a belt of minstrel halls developed, extending from Fellow's Opera House at 444 Broadway between Howard and Grand streets, to a hall in the converted Hope Chapel just south of Waverly Place.[7] Between these two minstrel halls, just 10 blocks apart, legitimate theatres as well as minstrel houses were clustered, in marked contrast to the scattered pattern of past decades.[8] This concentration of theatres within a relatively small area was a significant advance in the development of a full-fledged entertainment center.

While popular entertainment was developing and theatres were beginning to settle on Broadway in growing numbers, the economic structure of the American theatre was undergoing a radical change—one which by 1900 would transform the theatre from an art form into a commercial enterprise—show business, as it came to be called.[9] At mid-century, the longstanding stock company, a continuous producing unit which was functionally independent, usually attached to a specific theatre, and rotated its bill nightly, was being replaced as the basic producing unit by the traveling combination company. Combination companies were formed by stars or managers for only one play and, "instead of being localized as were stock companies, [were] organized in a producing center, generally New York, where they remain[ed] while they [could] attract profitable audiences, after which they visit[ed] the available theatres throughout the country."[10] Once a production had exhausted its audiences in New York and on the road, the company was disbanded. It is essentially the same system that still operates in the commercial theatre today.

The breakdown of stock and the rise of the combination system created a need for a new industry, the theatrical support industry, which began to emerge in the middle decades of the nineteenth century. Unlike the stock company, which produced its own scenery, costumes, and properties "on site," the combination company had neither staff nor facilities to provide these needs. To fill this void, enterprising businessmen founded specialized businesses (scenery, costume, and props shops) equipped to build the increasingly complex spectacular scenery and the magnificent costumes demanded by the growing number of combination companies. With a growing proportion of the acting profession unattached to a specific company and frequently "at liberty," a demand for the professional talent broker, the agent, was also being created. Increased competition, the result of a more speculative economic climate, generated the need for more publicity and brought increased business to the theatrical printer and the bill poster. The growing demand for the latest plays by both managers and a more theatrically aware public, prompted entrepreneurs to specialize in the publishing and selling of playscripts. It was the coalescence of these enterprises in one area, Union Square, during the 1870s and 1880s that distinguished New York's first modern theatrical center from the earlier concentration of theatres on Broadway between Howard and Waverly streets.

The distinction of being New York's first theatrical center was due in part to chance. Not only was Union Square the geographical center of the city in 1870, it also was situated at the junction of Broadway and the Bowery, seats of past theatrical activity. As theatres and early support businesses followed the northward movement of the city, they naturally funneled into the square. Its location on a major cross-town route guaranteed its accessibility from all directions, a factor that had prompted many first-class hotels and restaurants to settle in the area years before theatres located there. The erection in the 1870s of elevated railroad lines on 3rd and 6th avenues, near the eastern and western boundaries of the Rialto respectively, further increased the square's accessibility. By the end of its tenure as a theatrical center in the late nineties, even the inhabitants of the northernmost regions of Manhattan and the other boroughs could ride to the theatre by rail.

The movement of theatres and support business into the Union Square area also coincided with the emergence of specialized commercial districts in New York, as particular trades came to dominate specific sectors of the city:

> Wall Street was lined with financial offices and bank buildings. The Merchants' Exchange between William and Hanover was the headquarters for stock trading. Wholesale grocers were on Front Street; hat and fur dealers on Water Street; the leather interests on Ferry Street; clothing shops on Catherine and Cherry.[11]

The section of Broadway from A. T. Stewart's mammoth emporium, between 9th and 10th streets, to 23rd St. became the fashionable shopping district, known as the "Ladies' Mile," and 14th St. was the city's and the nation's piano capital, appropriately dubbed "Piano-forte-eenth Street." With commercial districting a city-wide pattern by the 1870s, New Yorkers readily accepted Union Square as their theatrical center.

By then it already had a rich and varied history. Originally named Union Place, the square had existed on paper since 1811, when the Randel Plan, which created the present grid pattern of streets and avenues above Houston St., was adopted, but there had been no attempt to build a public park there until 1831. During the intervening 20 years, the area remained relatively unspoiled, with farm houses and barns sharing the landscape with two country inns, the Norway House and the Rip Van Winkle Inn. Crude squatters' shanties and vegetable patches surrounded a small pond and nearby stood a powder house and a branch of the Bank of Manhattan, built in 1822 when an epidemic of yellow fever prompted many to escape the lower regions of the island.

In 1831, local property owners began to agitate for improvements on the area, demanding the creation of the public park promised by the Randel Plan. Spurred by pressure from the landowners, the Common Council began legal proceedings in April 1831 to acquire the necessary land, and, on April 5 of the following year, the state legislature passed an enabling act for the clearing of the area. The park was laid out as an ellipse, 656 ft. at its longest point and 292 ft. at its widest. The design was influenced by the Rue de la Paix and the Place Vendôme in Paris.[12]

Although the park remained unfinished until the early 1840s, the improvements in the area attracted the attention of speculators and wealthy citizens interested in moving north from the then-fashionable areas surrounding Astor Place and Washington Square. One of the first to sense the potential of the Union

Place area was Samuel B. Ruggles, a founder of the Bank of Commerce. In May 1834 Ruggles leased a number of lots on the east side of the park and constructed a row of elegant, four-story brownstone mansions. By 1841, Ruggles' speculation began to pay dividends: lots that had sold for $500 in 1831 were worth 10 times that amount in 1841. In the years that followed, New York's social elite competed with each other for the privilege of moving into one of Ruggles' houses; by 1845 Union Place had become the city's most exclusive residential neighborhood, resembling the fashionable Belgravia district near London's Hyde Park.

The area's reputation as the Belgravia of New York was fully justified. By the mid-forties, the plot of land that just 50 years before had been a forsaken wasteland, had been reshaped into a ''handsome oval of greenery . . . provided with excellent shrubbery and trees,'' enclosed within a high, iron fence (fig. 2).[13] Four entrances, each flanked by tall pillars topped with two stone cannonballs and equipped with heavy gates, gave access to the park. At sundown each evening, the gates were locked because, according to city officials, nighttime was no time for the enjoyment of parks.

In 1842 a magnificent iron fountain at the center of the park was dedicated and first operated as part of a city-wide celebration of the opening of the Croton Aqueduct. From the fountain at the center, tree-lined gravel walks radiated to the outer perimeter of the park; benches and stone seats were liberally distributed throughout. From the beginning, the park was a popular gathering place for the residents of the area—businessmen spending a lunch hour in the sun, nursemaids wheeling baby carriages, and small children playing in or near the fountain.

Henry James, whose family lived at 58 W. 14th St. between 1848 and 1855, recalled, in an interview after he became a famous author, playing near the fountain as a child and being chased from the vicinity by ''an aged amateur-looking constable, awful to my generation in virtue of his star and his switch.''[14] Years later, the same fountain (now stocked with goldfish) became a ''stage'' for actor George Holland. Dressed in ''sporting clothes'' and seated on a camp stool, Holland began to earnestly fish in the fountain, attracting a sizable crowd. Holland's fishing expedition continued to the delight of his audience, until the police ended the activity.[15]

After mid-century, businessmen and residents continued to improve the park and the surrounding area. In 1856, a statue of George Washington on horseback was erected by city merchants outside the park on the exact spot (on 4th Ave.) where Washington was received by the citizenry on Evacuation Day in 1783. The Washington statue was joined in 1868 by one of Abraham Lincoln, paid for by popular subscription. In 1876, French residents of New York erected a statue of Lafayette ''as a token of gratitude for American sympathy in the Franco-Prussian War.''[16]

During the 1840s and 1850s, the solid Victorian brownstones on the park and on W. 14th St. remained the most desirable residences in the city, and a list of

Figure 2. Union Square at Mid-Century. Viewed from the southern end of the park. (*Courtesy of the Theatre Collection, Museum of the City of New York*)

the area's residents was a veritable social register of the times. The list, which included such names as Vanderbilt, de Forest, Huntington, Whitney, Roosevelt, and de Peyster, represented Wall Street, international commerce, banking, merchandising, the professions, and long-established first families.

When the wealthy moved into the Union Place area, they were quickly followed by the institutions that served them—churches, private schools, expensive restaurants, private clubs, museums, and art galleries. Union Place was home of the Spingler Institute, the Misses Gibson's School for Ladies, and Dr. Abbot's School. The prestigious Union League Club established its headquarters on the west side of the park, while the equally exclusive Century Club was situated across Union Place. By 1855, the Bryan Gallery of Christian Art on Broadway just below 14th St. "was visited daily by . . . prominent and cultured men of business."[17] Many of these gentlemen were later instrumental in founding the Metropolitan Museum of Art, which had its second home in the former Douglass Mansion at 126-30 W. 14th St. Among the cultural institutions established in the 1850s were the area's first theatres—the Academy of Music, the city's new home of grand opera, erected at the northeast corner of Irving Place and 14th St. in 1854, and Dodworth Hall, a concert-lecture hall at 806-808 Broadway, opened in the same year.[18]

During the late 1840s and early 1850s, several of the hotels that would later serve theatrical clientele were constructed. In 1848, the Union Place Hotel was opened in a converted three-story mansion on the south side of the park between Broadway and 4th Ave. The hotel contained a fashionable French restaurant, the Maison Dorée, which was popular with the neighborhood's wealthy. The Union Place Hotel was joined early in the 1850s by the St. Denis at Broadway and 11th St., the Clarendon at 18th St. and 4th Ave., and the Everett House on the northern border of the park at 17th St.

During the 1860s, as the wealthy abandoned Union Place for 5th Ave. and Gramercy Park, businesses previously excluded from the area began to open. In 1858, R. H. Macy and Company became the first retail store in the area, opening a "minuscule shop" on 6th Ave. and 14th St. Eight years later, the retail trades moved into the square itself. In May 1866, C. A. Stevens and Company, Silversmiths, moved from the corner of Broadway and Broome St. to new quarters on the south side of 14th St., directly opposite the park. Stevens was followed shortly thereafter by W. F. Sherwin's dry goods emporium in the former Maison Dorée and Henry Maillard's confectionary shop on the northwest corner of Broadway and 14th St.[19] By 1868, A. T. Stewart had opened his store at Broadway and 9th St., soon to be unofficially designated the southern end of Ladies' Mile; many other retail stores were leasing the ground floors of neighborhood brownstones vacated by the wealthy who had moved uptown; and the first theatrical business in the area, the Eaves Costume Company, had opened just two blocks south of 14th St.

While businesses were moving into the Union Square area in the 1860s, so, too, were new places of amusement. The Palace Gardens, a pleasure garden, had opened in the late fifties at 6th Ave. and 14th St. and was at the height of its popularity in the early sixties; Irving Hall, a concert-lecture hall on the southwest corner of Irving Place and 15th St. was built in 1860; and Wallack's Theatre, the New York home of refined British comedy, was erected at Broadway and 13th St. the following year. By the end of the decade, the neighborhood contained the Fourteenth Street Theatre, on 14th St. west of 6th Ave.; the Hippotheatron, an amphitheatre erected opposite the Academy of Music; Steinway Hall, a third concert-lecture theatre, on E. 14th St. just west of the Academy; Bryant's Minstrel Hall and the Tammany Variety Palace, both situated in Tammany Hall at 141 E. 14th St.; and several smaller theatres.

In 1870, with the opening of the Union Square Theatre, which for more than a decade would be the home of A. M. Palmer's famous stock company, Union Square became generally recognized as the city's entertainment center. Four years later it was officially dubbed the Rialto by Ted McAlpin, a reporter for the *New York Sun*. For the next 30 years—a period in theatrical history characterized by the artistic experimentation of Saxe-Meiningen, Wagner, Zola, and Lugné-Poë and others in Europe, and the creation of the Theatrical Syndicate, the United Booking Office, and the final commercialization of the theatre in America—the square remained the hub of New York's and the country's theatrical activity until it was eclipsed by Times Square, the current Rialto, at the end of the nineteenth century.

2

Opera on Fourteenth Street:
The Academy of Music

Although Union Square would not become the center of theatrical activities in New York until the late 1860s, the Rialto had its beginnings in 1854 with the building of the Academy of Music. The Academy was the fourth theatre erected for the express purpose of presenting grand opera in New York and the first to achieve any measure of success or longevity. The Italian Opera House, at the intersection of Church and Leonard streets (1833-35), and Palmo's Opera House on Chambers St. (1844-45), both lasted only two seasons and resulted in the financial ruin of their managers. The third, the Astor Place Opera House, built in 1847, saw its reputation permanently tarnished by the Astor Place riot in 1849 and ended its days as a theatre in 1852 housing dog shows and menageries.

In 1852, while the Astor Place Opera House was still in its death throes, a corporation headed by Leonard W. Jerome, H. G. Stebbins, and P. C. Schuyler was formed "to provide a more luxurious structure than anything yet contemplated in this country."[1] Toward this goal, the corporation raised $195,000 of the $200,000 projected cost of the Academy of Music through a combination of public and private subscription. It purchased a plot of land at the northeast corner of 14th St. and Irving Place from James Phalen for $60,000, and hired Alexander Saeltzer, a German architect, to design the structure. At the same time, Signor Allegri of New York was engaged to provide the decorations of the auditorium, including the dome, drop curtain, scenery, and stage machinery. When construction was completed, the total cost of the new house had exceeded the initial estimate by $135,000.[2]

At the time, the Academy was the largest theatre in New York and one of the largest in the world. It extended 104 ft. on Irving Place, 204 ft. on 14th St., and was 86 ft. high, dwarfing the three- and four-story buildings that surrounded it. The exterior (fig. 3) was chocolate-colored stone accented by dark window sashes and topped with a heavy ornamental balustrade. Two entrances gave access to the house, one on Irving Place, the other on 14th St., each equipped with globe lamps overhead. A low iron fence flanked the sidewalks.

Figure 3.   The Academy of Music.
(Courtesy of the Billy Rose Theatre Collection, New York Public Library)

While the exterior of the Academy was commonly described as imposing, but plain, the interior (fig. 4), "though lacking the grandeur and magnificence of Covent Garden, or the more gentle beauty" of Her Majesty's Opera House, was universally regarded as impressive.[3] Once past the ticket-taker and through the "ample" lobby, the patron entered into what one critic described as "that vast and splendid void." The auditorium, which rose to a height of 80 ft. at the tip of the dome, accommodated 4,600 people and was in the shape of a horseshoe. It was divided into a parquet (equivalent to today's orchestra), a dress circle slightly elevated from the parquet, three tiers of seats supported by massive iron pillars above the dress circle, and 18 private proscenium boxes (9 on each side of the auditorium).[4]

According to the critic for the *Times,* the parquet, dress circle (also called the balcony), and the second and third tiers together seated roughly 2,200 in iron chars with velvet cushions. These chairs, designed by A. H. Allen of Boston, were considered unique at the time because they were equipped with springs and automatically folded up when not in use. The fourth tier, which at the Academy was termed the "amphitheatre," accommodated 1,800 persons in leather-cushioned seats said to be unusually comfortable for gallery seats. The remaining 600 seats were located in family boxes, similar to those at Niblo's Garden, at the rear of the first and second tiers, and in the proscenium boxes.[5]

While the entire theatre drew considerable attention from the press, the main focus was on the private boxes. The proscenium boxes were equipped with conventional chairs and were both elegant and spacious. The balcony boxes just above the parquet had "bannister fronts painted white, with red velvet cushions."[6] These were paneled and decorated with small statues of cherubs playing musical instruments set in niches, while the second tier boxes were embossed with lyres. Those on the third tier were without decoration. Above the third tier were four pigeon-like boxes, called Shakespeare boxes.

The most important feature of the private boxes, however, was the opportunity they provided their inhabitants for being seen. As in Covent Garden, the boxes were built out and were "only separated from one another by a low partition, so that their occupants [could] see all around and about them."[7] To the members of New York's aristocracy who went to the Academy to certify their social status, this feature was far more significant than whether they had the best seats for viewing the opera.

The entire auditorium was painted in gold and white, accentuated by more than 100 gas burners spread throughout the house. The dome of the auditorium, 80 ft. above the parquet floor, appeared flat and without any visible means of support. It was decorated with beautifully rendered paintings of Music, Tragedy, Comedy, and Poetry designed and executed by Signor Allegri. Suspended from the center of the dome, a magnificent chandelier threw "a rim of fire up over head encircling the base of the dome."[8]

Although the new theatre was a triumph, both aesthetically and acoustically, it was not without flaws. The gas burners on the proscenium boxes obscured the

Figure 4.   Interior of the Academy of Music.
(Ballou's Pictorial Drawingroom Companion)

vision of some spectators on the sides of the house, and the orchestra pit was not deep enough, causing the tops of the double basses or the heads of taller musicians to obstruct the sightlines of patrons in the parquet. The iron columns obliterated the view of still others.[9] In all, it was impossible to see the entire stage clearly from almost one-quarter of the seats in the house. At the time the Academy opened, many patrons sarcastically joked that not even a giraffe would have been able to see around some of the corners in the auditorium. By the end of the first season, the management was forced to remove 1,100 seats to placate irate ticket holders.

While there was widespread criticism of the seating, no one found fault with the stage, which, at the time, was one of the largest and best equipped in the world. The proscenium opening was 44 ft. wide, 40 ft. high, and the stage extended 66 ft. from the footlights to the back wall. The stage house rose to a height of 70 ft., the depth beneath the stage was 14 ft., and wing space was 36 ft. at the first four entrances and 76 ft. at the fifth and sixth entrances.[10] The stage was equipped with six traps, a bridge at the back, and an "immense" scene room for Signor Allegri and his assistants.

As the Academy's first impresario the Board of Directors selected Max Maretzek, who had served in the same capacity at the Astor Place Opera House. Maretzek sublet the theatre to J. H. Hackett, who, at the time, was managing Mario, Marchese de Candia, the greatest tenor of the era, and Julia Grisi, an equally renowned soprano. With the onset of cold weather, Hackett was eager to find a new house for the Mario-Grisi Company, which was then appearing at the unheated Castle Garden. He was quick to sense that opening the magnificent new Academy with his stars offered a unique opportunity to realize a substantial profit.

For the Academy's debut on October 2, 1854, Hackett selected Bellini's *Norma* and, believing "that the occasion, offering as it did the new house, the famous singers, and a popular opera" warranted it, charged as much as had been charged for Jenny Lind's concerts in 1850-51.[11] Seats in the parquet, dress circle, second, and third tiers were $3.00, a seat in the amphitheatre was 50ᶜ and proscenium boxes were sold for $12 to $40. The public, regarding the prices as exorbitant, rebelled. Fewer than 1,500 people attended the opening, with the majority purchasing the cheaper seats. The following day, the newspapers unanimously condemned Hackett's attempt to line his pockets at the public's expense. Hackett, responding to the public outcry, promptly reduced prices for the second night to $2.00 for the parquet and dress circle and to $1.00 for the second and third tiers.

Hackett and his company continued until December 29, presenting *Lucrezia Borgia, La Sonnambula, Semiramide,* and *The Barber of Seville* and losing $8,000 before relinquishing the lease. The next lessee was Ole Bull, the famed Norwegian violinist, who reopened the theatre on February 19, 1855, presenting Beagio Bolcioni and Ettore Barili in *Rigoletto.* This venture was such a failure that Bull was forced to terminate his management after only two weeks. After Bull vacated the theatre, the stockholders took charge and presented the LaGrange Operatic Company for a short season. The new company, however, fared no better than had

Hackett and Bull, losing $12,000. Finally, in desperation, the stockholders hired Chevalier Wikoff to present yet another series of operas which resulted in the additional loss of $28,000. In all, the Academy lost more than $50,000 between October 1854 and June 1855.[12]

In an article published in 1855, Maretzek outlined the reasons for the first season's deficit and predicted that future managers would continue to lose money because of a provision in the Academy's charter. Anyone who owned one share of stock was entitled to a seat for the entire season and owners of four or more shares were granted a box for each performance. Thus, for a one-time investment of $1,000 per share, each shareholder was given $159.50 worth of tickets each season for each share held. These tickets were transferrable to friends and relatives who would have, under normal conditions, purchased tickets at the box office.[13] Added to the annual rent of $24,000, the monopoly of the best seats in the house resulted in a loss of revenue that virtually guaranteed a manager's financial failure. Artists who performed at the Academy knew of the institution's economic instability and frequently demanded to be paid in advance. In 1857, for example, the entire male chorus of *The Barber of Seville* refused to sing unless it received its salary before going on stage.

The Academy was a failure in another respect. As originally conceived by its founders, New York's new opera house, which was based upon the Académie Nationale de Musique in Paris, was to be an academy of music in fact as well as name. According to its charter, "the purposes of the Academy were set down as the cultivation of taste by entertainments accessible at moderate prices, by furnishing facilities for instruction and by rewards."[14] In short, the new institution was to include a conservatory to train American singers, musicians, and composers and to sponsor regular competitions to reward excellence. During his tenure as manager, Ole Bull announced that he would open the conservatory and offered a $1,000 prize for the "best original grand opera by an American composer, and upon a strictly American subject."[15] Unfortunately, before his plans could be augmented, Bull resigned and there were no further attempts to achieve the educational goals stated in the charter.

The debacle of the previous season and the restrictions of the charter notwithstanding, Maretzek optimistically opened the 1855-56 season on October 1 with two of the strongest attractions from the previous year: *Il Trovatore*, which had been performed for the first time in the United States at the Academy on April 30 with the popular Brignoli as Manrico, and Rossini's *Semiramide*, which also had its American premiere on the Academy stage. Prices had been standardized at $1.00 for the parquet and dress circle, 50ᶜ for the second and third tiers and 25ᶜ for the amphitheatre. For the Saturday matinee, any seat in the house (except stockholders' boxes) could be purchased for 50ᶜ. As had been hoped, the two popular operas at reduced prices increased attendance and, while still not yielding a profit, at least allowed Maretzek to reduce the operating deficit.

After the 1855-56 season, with seating problems solved and prices stabilized, the Academy settled into a routine of Italian and German opera. Between 1855 and 1858, Maretzek alternated as impresario with Maurice Strakosch and Bernard Ullman, and during this time *La Traviata* had its American premiere. Audiences at the Academy during the first four seasons witnessed world-class talents, including not only Mario and Grisi, but Brignoli, Adelaide Phillips, Maria Piccolomini, Karl Formes, Beagio Bolcioni, and Ettore Barili.

On November 24, 1859, the Academy was the site of an historic event in the operatic world, the debut of Adelina Patti. The daughter of well-known tenor Salvatore Patti, and the sister-in-law of Maurice Strakosch, Patti by the age of 16 had received extensive training and had been singing concerts since she was a child. When Strakosch encountered financial difficulties as impresario in 1859, he decided to present his young sister-in-law as Lucia in *Lucia di Lammermoor,* although he realized that she might not yet be ready for the rigors of a career in opera. Being cautious, however, he scheduled her debut for an "off night," Thanksgiving eve, when the majority of subscribers would be home preparing for the holiday.

When the reviews appeared the following day, Strakosch's worries proved unwarranted. The *Herald* noted that "she sang perfectly, displaying a thorough Italian method and a high soprano voice, fresh and full throughout," and executed a high E-flat with the greatest ease.[16] The critic from the *Times* raved, "In a debutante we do not look for the perfection which we now find in Adelina Patti . . . . Her powers of execution and her voice both in compass and quality, are of the first class."[17] Propelled to instant stardom, Patti continued to the end of the season, appearing in *La Sonnambula, The Huguenots, Ernani,* and *Don Giovanni.* By the end of her first year as a professional, she was the dominant figure on the American operatic stage and two years later she had become an international celebrity.

While the principal function of the Academy was the staging of grand opera, the managers and stockholders realized as early as 1855 that it would be necessary to increase revenues by renting the theatre for other forms of entertainment. Soon after the Academy opened, opera was forced to share the stage with popular entertainments, balls, benefits, and the spoken drama. Some of these so-called "minor" forms of performance became famous, equalling or surpassing in historical importance many of the operas.

The first popular entertainments were presented in the fall of 1855 when Maretzek sublet the house to John Brougham, who staged *Rip Van Winkle, The Kentuckian,* and, with Henry C. Jarrett, a matinee performance of *The Drunkard.* In May 1857 the burlesque, *Jenny Lind,* appeared on the same bill with Campbell's Minstrels, and in September 1861 Professor Karl Herrmann, the famed magician, presented a series of "prestidigitorial evenings" assisted by his wife and brother. Other prominent popular entertainments that appeared at the Academy included George L. Fox and Company in an aerial act titled "Zampillaero-station"

(1862), *Uncle Tom's Cabin* with Mrs. George C. Howard as Topsy (1867), Dan Bryant in *Handy Ande* (1870), and Lydia Thompson and her burlesque company (1873).

During the first 20 years of the theatre's existence, many historic performances of the classics were also mounted on the Academy's stage. In 1855, Edwin Booth made the first of many appearances when he and E. L. Davenport assumed the title roles in *Damon and Pythias*. Booth next appeared in March 1861 as Macbeth with Charlotte Cushman as Lady Macbeth, and again in September 1869 playing Iago opposite John McCullough's Othello. In 1866 the Academy was selected as the site of the farewell performance of Mr. and Mrs. Charles Kean in *Louis XI*, and later in the season Booth returned as Hamlet with Ida Vernon as the Queen. The following year Fanny Janauschek made her American debut at the Academy, as did Tommaso Salvini in 1873.

In 1876, the Academy hosted a performance of *Hamlet*, which achieved notoriety for an unusual reason. The theatre had been rented by Count Joannes, an extremely inept actor, and a large crowd had bought tickets to hoot, ridicule, and pelt the count with fruit and vegetables. When mayhem erupted early in the performance, Joannes stepped to the footlights and exhorted the audience, "Remember this is the Academy of Music. Prove yourselves gentlemen."[18] The audience quieted immediately and the performance continued without incident.

The theatre was also the site of benefits honoring J. W. Wallack, Tony Pastor, Dan Bryant, Lester Wallack, and Tony Hart, as well as performances for local charities. As was the custom of the period, actors donated their services for these benefits, often resulting in a vast array of celebrities on the same stage. One such performance took place at the Academy on November 1, 1877, at a benefit for the Roman Catholic Orphan Asylum during which Edwin Booth, E. A. Sothern, John McCullough, George Holland, Harry Lacy, J. H. Stoddard, Agnes Booth, John Gilbert, James O'Neill, Eben Plympton, Clara Morris, Rose Coughlan, Frank Mayo, Maude Granger, and F. F. Mackay appeared in different scenes from great plays.

When the parquet was cleared of seats and a floor laid down, the Academy became the largest ball-room in the city, with a dance floor more than 9,000 feet square. The theatre was the location of annual balls given by the Patriarchs, the Assembly, the Old Guard, The Arion, the French Cooks, and the Cercle de l'Harmonie, as well as the "Grand Reception and Ball" sponsored each year by the stockholders. These affairs were regularly attended by the New York press, and drawings frequently appeared in illustrated newspapers such as *Harper's Weekly, Frank Leslie's Illustrated Newspaper,* or *Ballou's Pictorial* (fig. 5), showing the dance floor crowded with participants while onlookers watched from the tiers above or from banquettes on the edge of the floor. When the event was too large for the Academy alone, the adjoining Nilsson Hall on 14th St., or Irving Hall, which was connected to the Academy by a tunnel under Irving Place, was utilized.

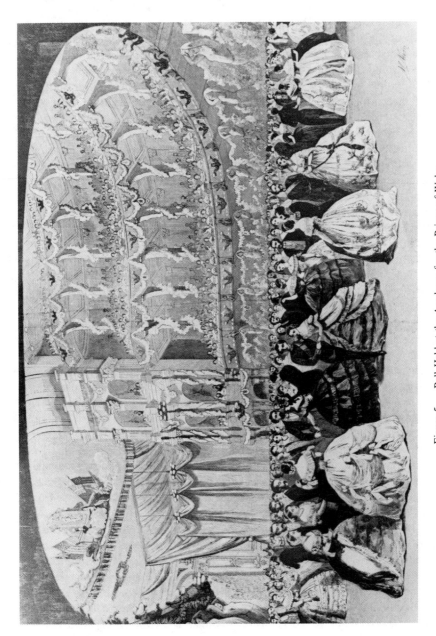

Figure 5.   Ball Held at the Academy for the Prince of Wales.
(Harper's Weekly)

The most famous ball at the Academy was held in October 1860 when the Prince of Wales visited New York. Two nights after his arrival, the city's first families entertained the prince at a mammoth reception at the Academy that was regarded as the social event of the decade. On the evening of the ball, the *Herald* had stationed a battalion of runners at the theatre to carry detailed accounts of the prince's actions to the newspaper's offices on Park Row. At 10:15 p.m. the first runner left the Academy with the news that the prince had arrived; from that time until 6:00 a.m. when the ball ended, a messenger sped off every 10 minutes with the latest report.

The evening's festivities were marred, however, by an unfortunate accident. As more than 4,000 persons crowded onto the floor for the first dance of the night, it collapsed—or as *Harper's Weekly* reported, sank several feet. Two dancers were thrown into the basement, but were miraculously uninjured. Fortunately, Isaac Brown, the Academy's major-domo (also the sexton of Grace Church), had foreseen such an occurrence and had stationed the theatre's stagehands in the cellar. Brown's army of stagehands quickly raised the floor manually, braced it with timbers, and the ball continued.[19]

During the first half of the 1860s, when the Academy was alternately managed by Maretzek and Jacob Grau, the seasons were shortened because of the war. With the exception of Clara Louise Kellogg, who made her debut as Gilda on February 27, 1861, the singers were second rate. Adelina Patti was in Europe and foreign stars were reluctant to venture to a war-torn country to appear in half-filled houses. Those who did come to the United States demanded to be paid in advance in gold, causing the managers further hardship. Reluctantly, at the beginning of the 1864-65 season, Maretzek, responding to the economic crisis, raised the prices of seats in the parquet from $1.00 to $1.50, apologizing to his patrons in a program insert.

The following season (1865-66) began on a discordant note and ended in disaster. When Maretzek opened his season, he was promptly and viciously attacked by the *Herald*, which suggested that he was cheating the public by presenting inferior singers at inflated prices. Maretzek responded by placing ads in rival newspapers labeling the *Herald* management "deadheads" and persuading other theatre managers to join him in an advertising boycott of the paper. The feud lasted the entire season and was only resolved when the newspaper agreed to refrain from such personal attacks in the future.[20]

The season ended abruptly on May 21, 1866, when the Academy burned to the ground. Shortly after a performance of *La Juive,* presented by Jacob Grau, stagehands discovered a fire under the stage. In an effort to control the blaze, they ripped up the stage floor and poured buckets of water into the basement. By the time the fire department arrived, however, the entire theatre was in flames, and an hour and a half after the fire started, the interior had been totally destroyed. It was a heavy loss to the stockholders, who had insured the $350,000 building for only $180,000; to Grau, who lost the scenery and costumes for *La Juive*; and to Maretzek, who lost the music of more than 50 operas as well as costumes and scenery.[21]

Indirectly, the fire contributed to a landmark in American theatre history—the creation of *The Black Crook*. Prior to the fire, Harry Jarrett and Henry C. Palmer had booked the Academy to present *La Biche au Bois*, a ballet-extravaganza featuring dancers, costumes, and "trick" scenery imported from Europe. The troupe and its costumes and scenery had already arrived in New York when the Academy burned, and Jarrett and Palmer, unable to book another theatre, faced losing the entire investment. To avoid such a loss, they sold the dancers' contracts and the scenic elements to William Wheatley, manager of Niblo's Garden, who at the time was planning to stage *The Black Crook*, a flimsy melodrama based upon the Faust legend. Fearing that a straightforward production of the play would lose money, Wheatley seized the opportunity to inject the spectacular elements offered to him by Jarrett and Palmer into his production. When the "improved" *Black Crook* opened on September 16, 1866, it was an immediate sensation, running for 475 performances in 16 months and returning in excess of $1 million to Wheatley.[22]

The Academy was rebuilt within the original shell by architect Thomas R. Jackson and reopened on March 1867 with a benefit for Maretzek designed to express sympathy for his losses in the fire. Opera was resumed the same month, with Kellogg, Mazzoleni, Ronconi, and Antonucci appearing in the *Barber of Seville*. The Academy now entered a "golden period" that was to continue until the early 1880s. With Maretzek, Grau, and Strakosch alternating as manager, the theatre attained the highest level of financial stability in its history. The Academy was the site of the American premieres of *Aida* (1873), *Lohengrin* (1874), *Die Walküre* (1877), and *Carmen* (1878), and was home to many international stars. In addition to Kellogg, Brignoli, and Anna Louise Cary, who regularly sang at the opera house in the early 1870s, Mme Parepa-Rosa appeared in May of 1870 in the *Marriage of Figaro*. Two years later, she made her final New York appearance at the Academy in the role of Valentine in *Les Huguenots*. The most significant event of this era, however, was the American debut of Christine Nilsson, who was billed as the successor to her countrywoman, Jenny Lind.

Col. James H. Mapleson joined the managerial staff of the Academy in 1875 and assumed full control in 1878, beginning a regime that lasted until 1885. Near the end of the seventies, with the annual deficit again increasing and talk of building a new opera house uptown becoming widespread, Mapleson was the ideal choice for the Academy's impresario. A personable and persuasive Englishman, Mapleson was able to obtain favors and concessions that allowed the theatre to continue operating in financially difficult times. According to legend, Adelina Patti, who was known for her acquisitive nature and a shrewd, almost ruthless, business sense, waived her customary payment-in-advance rule for Mapleson.

In 1882, internal discontent erupted into a full-scale battle for control of opera in New York. The Academy had withstood a challenge to its supremacy from Pike's Opera House in 1868, but the new threat to its position grew from within the ranks of its most influential patrons and was focused upon one of the few serious flaws in the theatre's physical structure: the scarcity of private boxes. The Academy's 18 boxes were as exclusive as seats on the stock exchange and were completely controlled by old-guard Knickerbocker society. By 1880, the "old-line" aristocracy's monopoly of the best seats in the Academy was being challenged by "the then *nouveau-riche*, consisting of such nabobs as Jay Gould, J. P. Morgan, Cornelius Vanderbilt, William Whitney . . . and William Rockefeller" who were frustrated in their repeated attempts to purchase the prized boxes, even though upwards of $25,000 had been offered.[23] When a compromise solution of constructing 26 additional boxes was rejected by the Academy's Board of Directors in 1882, New York's budding aristocracy formed a corporation to build its own opera house uptown. Once finished, the Metropolitan Opera House, which one critic termed the "Yellow Brewery on Broadway," had 122 private boxes, ample space for all of the "new upstart millionaires."[24]

Backed by a practically unlimited supply of money and administered by Henry E. Abbey, one of New York's shrewdest managers, the new opera house immediately began bidding for the services of the world's best singers. Abbey opened the Metropolitan on October 22, 1883, with a performance of *Faust* featuring one of the strongest casts ever assembled in the city (Campanini, Novara, Del Puente, Sofia Scalchi, and Christine Nilsson); he strengthened his position by signing Campanini, Nilsson, and the Polish contralto, Marcella Sembrich, to long-term contracts. Mapleson, sensing battle, retaliated by signing Patti, Emma Nevada, and Etelka Gerster, the Hungarian coloratura "who astonished [audiences] by touching high F twice in one evening."[25] For two seasons, the opera war continued, with Abbey relying heavily upon Nilsson and Sembrich, matching Mapleson's regular presentation of Patti and Gerster, and each house promising more than the other in the daily newspapers. While the night-to-night competition was a boon to opera lovers, it ultimately was fatal to the Academy. In the spring of 1885, Mapleson, stating simply that "I cannot fight Wall Street," finally admitted defeat and the Metropolitan became the city's official home of opera.

Mapleson resigned at the end of the 1884-85 season and Theodore Thomas, a prominent local orchestra leader, presented a short season of opera in English early in 1886. In April of the following year, the property was sold at auction to W. B. Dinsmore for $195,000 and later resold to W. P. Douglas for $325,000. In November 1887, Douglas leased the theatre to Eugene Tompkins and E. P. Gilmore, who converted the Academy into a combination house. Under Gilmore and Tompkins' management, the Academy became one of America's leading booking houses, hosting the best traveling companies in popular plays and the classics.

During the 23 years (1887-1910) that the Academy was a combination house, the most popular plays and actors of the era could be seen there. In December 1887, Edwin Booth and Lawrence Barrett starred in a production of *Julius Caesar*, which featured 200 supernumeraries on stage at once. Each spring E. H. Sothern and Julia Marlowe presented a repertory of Shakespeare on the stage where Sothern's father had once appeared as the immortal Dundreary in *Our American Cousin*. Beginning in August 1888, the theatre was monopolized by Denman

Figure 6.   The Academy of Music, 1916.
            (Courtesy of the Theatre Collection, Museum of the City of New York)

Thompson as the ever-popular Josh Whitcomb in his play *The Old Homestead*. Thompson's play continued for three seasons, temporarily establishing a new house record for a long run. In the 1890s, the Academy housed revivals of some of the most popular plays from past decades. During this period, *The Black Crook, Uncle Tom's Cabin, Shenandoah,* and *In Old Kentucky* were given new life on the Academy's stage. Opera was last heard at the theatre in March 1896 when Gilmore and Tompkins rented the house to the Damrosch Opera Company for a short season consisting of *Siegfried, Die Meistersinger, Tristan and Isolde,* and *Götterdämmerung.*

Gilmore and Tompkins' management and the Academy's reign as a major booking house ended in June 1910 with a production of *Hamlet* starring E. H. Sothern and Julia Marlowe. The theatre then passed into the hands of Corse Payton, a producer of 10-20-30ᶜ stock productions, and for 11 weeks housed cheap melodramas. When Payton vacated the theatre, it became a low-priced vaudeville house presenting "ferris wheel" or continuous shows at popular prices.

In 1912, William Fox, who was destined to become a giant in the film industry, leased the theatre, totally renovated it, and established the Academy of Music Stock Company to present melodrama. Shortly thereafter, Fox disbanded the company and converted the theatre into a movie house (fig. 6). The Academy continued to show films until it was purchased and razed in 1926 to make room for the Consolidated Edison office building. Closing ceremonies were held on May 17, 1926, and, with the singing of an aria from *Norma*, the doors to the Academy were closed forever.

3

Stock Companies on Union Square: Wallack's and the Union Square Theatre

By the time the Rialto became firmly entrenched on Union Square, the "combination" company headed by a major star was rapidly becoming the accepted unit of production, and the stock system, which had existed in this country for more than 50 years, was in decline. In 1871-72, there were 50 permanent stock companies operating in the United States; by 1880, only 7 or 8 remained. Three of the best—Augustin Daly's, Wallack's, and the Union Square Stock Company—were located in New York, with the latter two on Union Square.

Wallack's Theatre at the northeast corner of 13th St. and Broadway (fig. 7) was the second house to bear the Wallack name. The first, at the corner of Broome Street and Broadway, was built in 1850 by John Brougham; it was taken over two years later by J. W. Wallack and renamed Wallack's Lyceum. Once established in his own theatre, Wallack began creating a company that was unrivalled in excellence anywhere in the country. While Wallack maintained a stock company throughout his career and rejected the star system that was then becoming popular, many of the actors in his early company would later become stars on the American stage. In the nine years that Wallack remained in the Broome St. house, Laura Keene, E. A. Sothern, John Brougham, Matilda Heron, J. H. Stoddard, and Agnes Robertson were members of his troupe. With the best company in New York and taste, elegance, and propriety displayed in every production, Wallack's Lyceum soon challenged Burton's Theatre (regarded by many as the city's most popular theatre), ultimately becoming the city's leading theatre.

In 1861 Wallack moved his company to a new theatre at Broadway and 13th St., an audacious decision at the time since the center of theatrical activity was then still well below Union Square. The land selected for the site of the new house was owned by the Astor family and had been leased to William Gibson, "with the express understanding that no theatre should be built" there.[1] But Wallack, after negotiations with the Astors, finally obtained their permission to incorporate his theatre into the proposed Gibson Building.

The five-story Gibson Building with the theatre on the ground floor and offices for Wallack and his assistants on the floors above, was designed and constructed

Figure 7.   Wallack's Theatre (Renamed the Star Theatre in 1883).
(Courtesy of the Theatre Collection, Museum of the City of New York)

by architect Thomas R. Jackson on a lot that measured 75 ft. on Broadway by 148 ft. on 13th St. Inside, the auditorium was 95 by 72 ft. and accommodated 1,605 people, approximately 500 more than Wallack's Lyceum on Broome St. Two 20-foot wide entrances, one on Broadway and the other on 13th St. (fig. 8), met "in a roomy hall, from which radiated entrances into all parts of the house, affording easy access, and quick and ready egress in the case of fire."[2] A third entrance on 4th Ave. led through a long corridor to the stage and backstage areas.

Once inside the theatre and past the check-gate in the hall, three large doors directly ahead of the patron led to the parquet, while stairs to the left and right led to the family and dress circles. The auditorium (fig. 9) was divided into three price ranges: the orchestra chairs or stalls at the front of the ground floor, costing $1.00, were the most expensive and exclusive; the parquet chairs located behind the stalls sold for 50[c], as did seats in the first tier (called the dress circle or balcony). The least expensive seats (25[c]) were located in the second tier, which at Wallack's was termed the family circle or second balcony. "These two circles carried their sweep round the house, almost unbroken by private boxes."[3] The seats in the stalls, the parquet section, and the dress circle were lined and backed with velvet and were "much more comfortable than in most theatres, plenty of room being left between them," while in the family circle, deep banquettes had replaced the hard benches customarily found in theatre galleries.[4]

Each of the eight private proscenium boxes accommodated seven people and cost $7.00, but only the *nouveau riche* purchased boxes at Wallack's. The *haute monde* preferred the orchestra stalls because "according to the inscrutable tradition of New York, to take a box for the play was even more flagrantly bad form than not to take one for the opera."[5] Consequently, the private boxes at Wallack's were of secondary importance and little was written about them when the theatre opened.

The critics also paid little attention to the decoration of the new house, but were impressed with its size, comfort, and the restraint exhibited in its furnishings which were "modest and tasteful, the gaudy steamboat style being entirely eschewed."[6] Corridors, lobbies, and lounges were unusually spacious and well appointed, affording the theatre-goer ample opportunity to relax between the acts; and a men's café and smoking room in the basement provided liquor and cigars at modest prices. Because of its size, comfort, and simple beauty, Wallack's evoked favorable comparison with London's famed Drury Lane.

The stage was 80 ft. high, 50 ft. deep and had a proscenium opening 32 ft. wide and 40 ft. high. Forty feet of wing space was provided behind the curtain line and the depth under the stage was 10 ft. In equipping the theatre, "every modern device for perfecting the scenic illusion and concealing the machinist's art [was] adopted," and Wallack boasted that the shifting of scenery (of the traditional drop and wing variety) could be accomplished without any machinery or technicians being seen.[7] The stage was constructed without trapdoors, possibly because Wallack eschewed Shakespeare and melodramas that would require sudden spectacular "visitations" or disappearances.

Figure 8.   Wallack's Theatre Viewed from 4th Ave. The 13th St. entrance and the stage door.
(Courtesy of the Theatre Collection, Museum of the City of New York)

Figure 9.   Interior of Wallack's Theatre.
(Courtesy of the Theatre Collection, Museum of the City of New York)

Wallack inaugurated his new house on September 25, 1861 (the same night that Herrmann the Magician opened at the Academy of Music), with *The New President*, a comedy by Tom Taylor. The opening night had been sold out well in advance, and Wallack placed ads in the daily newspapers warning the public not to purchase tickets on the sidewalks outside the theatre and advising that there would "be no free list or complimentary admissions, except only the usual privileges of the press."[8] By 7:30, a delightful and fashionable audience with everyone in excellent humor had gathered and there was a general air of excitement and anticipation in the house, generated by the realization that the evening was both socially and theatrically important. Between the second and third acts, the elder Wallack welcomed the audience in what would be the last stage appearance of his life.

J. W. Wallack continued as nominal head of the company until his death in 1864, although the theatre was actually managed by his son. When the second house was opened, the elder Wallack charged his son, "I have made this organization a perfect stock company. You keep it so."[9] During the 1860s Lester Wallack continued to improve the company until it was widely regarded as one of the best in the world, said to be superior even to that of the Comédie Française.

While the excellence of the company, the high standard of production, and the reputation as a fashionable theatrical rendezvous would have been sufficient to ensure that the theatre would remain one of the best in America, the Wallacks consolidated their position by selecting a repertoire that was both "tasteful" and popular. The elder Wallack, in a curtain speech on the opening night of the first theatre, told his audience what sort of plays they might expect: "The style of our performance, ladies and gentlemen, will be high comedy [of] the highest and best class."[10] To the Wallacks, high comedy meant British comedy, both such time-tested favorites as *She Stoops to Conquer, School for Scandal,* and *The Rivals,* and contemporary English comedies.

Lester Wallack continued his father's devotion to British scripts and this preference became a characteristic of his management. Consequently, American playwrights, in general, failed to get their work produced at his theatre. Among the few exceptions to the British domination of Wallack's were *Twins* by the noted critic Nym Crinkle, and *Americans in Paris*, a farce by Henry Hurlbut. Bronson Howard nearly joined their select circle when Wallack agreed to produce *Shenandoah* if the setting were changed to the Crimea, but Howard refused to compromise and Wallack subsequently rejected the script.

Probably the only other script by an American to be produced at the 13th St. house was Wallack's own play, *Rosedale,* which opened on September 30, 1863, with the playwright in the role of Elliott Grey. The play was immensely popular, running for 125 performances with nightly receipts averaging an unprecedented $1,482.[11] After the initial production, *Rosedale* entered the repertoire and was successfully revived five times between 1864 and 1877.

While Wallack's customary fare of British high comedy remained popular until the late 1870s, *Rosedale* marked the introduction of romantic melodrama into the repertoire. The most popular production in the 37-year history of Wallack's, *The Shaughran* by Dion Boucicault, belonged to this subgenre. With the author in the leading role of Conn, and Harry Montague and Ada Dyas as the young lovers, *The Shaughran* opened November 11, 1874 and had 143 performances, earning $220,076.50 and estsablishing Harry Montague as America's first matinee idol.[12]

In 1874, the year *The Shaughran* opened, Wallack's company was as prestigious as ever; but during the next 10 years, its reputation gradually declined as the stalwarts of past years departed. The public tired of English comedies and attendance steadily diminished. Wallack reacted to the decline in two ways; he included more spectacular melodramas in the repertoire (*Moths, Forbidden Fruit, My Awful Dad*) and he began planning for a new theatre farther uptown.

In June 1881, Wallack allowed the lease on the theatre to lapse and moved his company to a new house at the corner of Broadway and 30th St. In September of the same year, the recently vacated Wallack's was leased to Adolph Neuendorff, who had run a German theatre from 1874 to 1881 in the small auditorium that was to achieve immortality as Tony Pastor's New Fourteenth Street Theatre. Renamed the Germania, the once renowned home of high comedy hosted one of the best German companies in the city for the next two years, and in March 1882 was filled to capacity by Adelina Patti in a season consisting of *Il Trovatore, Lucia di Lammermoor,* and *La Traviata.*

In 1882 the lease reverted to Wallack. Neuendorff continued in the theatre throughout the 1882-83 season, presenting German light opera; when the season ended, he retired from the entertainment business entirely. In March 1883, the house was renamed The Star Theatre and Theodore Moss, a former Wallack employee, was installed as manager. With Dion Boucicault in *Vice Versa,* the theatre began a brilliant decade as a booking house featuring many of the era's most famous and accomplished artists.

Moss's first full season began successfully in August 1883 with Lawrence Barrett as Lanciotto the Hunchback in George Boker's tragedy, *Francesca da Rimini.* Moss followed Barrett's successful run with the American debut of Henry Irving in *The Bells,* appearances by Helena Modjeska, Stuart Robson, W. H. Crane, Edwin Booth in a Shakespearean repertoire, and John McCullough's final New York stage appearance (in *Richard III*).

Between 1884 and 1892, the success of Moss's first season was matched as "a long list of notable players appeared, and a number of fine productions and revivals were given."[13] Irving returned several times, appearing with Ellen Terry in a repertoire of Shakespeare in 1884. Adelaide Ristori portrayed Lady Macbeth in January 1885; Joseph Jefferson brought *Rip Van Winkle* to the Star in 1887; *Shenandoah,* once rejected by Wallack, received its first performance in September of 1889; and the theatre was the site for the American debut of Benoît Constant Coquelin, as well as several "return" engagements by Sarah Bernhardt. When Moss relinquished the lease in 1892, the theatre, while lacking the prestige of the Wallack name, had nevertheless compiled a record of excellence matched by few other booking houses in the country.

When Moss ended his management, he sublet the theatre to a series of managers, including Neil Burgess, Walter Sanford, and R. M. Gulick & Co. Each, during his managership, endeavored to maintain the high standards of the past. In the last decade of the theatre's existence, Kate Claxton appeared in a revival of *The Two Orphans*, Mrs. John Drew played the Widow Warren in *The Road to Ruin*, and Jefferson returned as Rip Van Winkle. Increasingly, however, managers of the 1890s were forced to stage cheap, flashy melodramas to compete with nearby vaudeville houses. The theatre also became a popular house for troupes such as Fred Rider's Night Owl Burlesquers and the Lilliputians, a company composed entirely of midgets.

In 1901, the theatre slipped from existence, not with the ceremony and fanfare befitting the former home of America's best company, but "without so much as a cheer for an epitaph." When the curtain fell on the final performance of *The Man-O-War*, no one stepped onstage to make a passionate farewell speech and most of the audience simply exited. As the orchestra played "The Last Rose of Summer," the curtain was raised to reveal stagehands striking the set and several cast members lingering onstage. Finally, Thomas Shea, an actor, gave a short, impromptu speech about the management's lack of interest. Shea was joined onstage by photographer George C. Rockwood, who recounted some of the theatre's brighter moments, a piano was wheeled on, and the cast and remaining audience members sang "Auld Lang Syne" and "raised three cheers for the good old Star." Within a matter of weeks, the theatre had been razed, and construction of an office building had begun.[14]

The second of the famous companies on Union Square, A. M. Palmer's Union Square Stock Company, was housed in a theatre (fig. 10) that actually abutted Wallack's and for 10 years the two neighboring companies waged a friendly battle for supremacy. Twenty years younger than Wallack's renowned troupe, Palmer's company nevertheless gained a large and enthusiastic following.

The theatre was built in 1870 by businessman Sheridan Shook, who owned the Union Place Hotel (later the Morton House) located on the south side of the square between Broadway and 4th Ave. Wishing to incorporate a theatre into the hotel, Shook hired contractor H. M. Simons, who had also built Daly's Fifth Avenue Theatre, to remove the hotel's dining room in the center of the structure and construct a first-class theatre. "The theatre, erected in about three months' time, extended longitudinally from 14th St. deep into [the] property . . . occupying a ground area averaging about 45 by 140 ft."[15] The auditorium was reached by a long,

Figure 10. The Union Square Theatre.
(Courtesy of the Theatre Collection, Museum of the City of New York)

beautifully frescoed and brilliantly lighted vestibule which led from a spacious portico on 14th St. through the hotel to the theatre. A separate entrance on 4th Ave. gave access to the family circle.

Shook's theatre accommodated 1,200 in a parquet on the ground floor, a dress circle (first tier), and a gallery or family circle above that. The critic for the *Herald* noted that "owing to the smallness of the plot upon which the theatre had been erected the house is built very high, and the appearance of the family circle, which rises tier above tier, is exceedingly stiff backed."[16]

The auditorium (fig. 11) was horseshoe-shaped with every consideration given to providing each spectator with an excellent view of the stage. In the dress circle, "the horseshoe curve of the rail [had] been made to descend towards the edge with a graceful sweep" to avoid blocking the vision of those in the back of the section; the family circle was so steeply pitched that each "gallery god," although precariously perched near the top of the house, was guaranteed full view of the stage.[17]

Compared to the neighboring Wallack's, the Union Square Theatre was heavily ornamented. Many considered it one of the prettiest theatres in the city. The auditorium was painted white with circular gold fluting and was frescoed in a lavish style. The boxes were "ornamented with curious intricate work in Byzantine style, and delicate blues and pinks made to harmonize with the lustrous gilding."[18] The proscenium arch was painted maroon with a gold edging to simulate drapery, and figures from mythology appeared throughout the house. Above the auditorium was a dome "extending above the roof of the building with windows on all sides, which materially assist[ed] ventilation."[19]

For a theatre that was regarded as small, the stage was generally spacious. The distance from footlights to back wall was 35 ft., and between the side walls, 50 ft. The depth under the stage was 9 ft., and the height to the rigging was 70 ft., allowing even the highest scenery to be flown completely out of sight. The stage was equipped with a fly gallery 29 ft. above the stage floor and "the usual number of traps."[20] The dressing rooms were located beneath the stage.

The Union Square Theatre opened as a variety house, advertised as "The Model Temple of Amusement," on September 11, 1871, under the management of Robert W. Butler, formerly manager of the American Concert Hall, a concert saloon so famous that it was commonly known simply as "444," its address on Broadway. For two seasons, the Union Square remained one of New York's leading variety theatres. The opening night bill, which "revealed an effort to eclipse all previous shows of the kind," featured Marie Bonfanti in a ballet titled "Home of the Butterflies," the Martinetti-Ravel troupe in "Pat-a-Cake Baker's Man," an original pantomime, and the Mathews Family of gymnasts and acrobats.

After the departure of the opening night performers, Butler maintained the high quality of the bill by presenting artists of the calibre of Harrigan and Hart, Gus Williams, the Wallhalla Troupe in an act called "The Prismatic Fountain," Bonfanti in several return engagements, and in April 1872 the American debut

Figure 11.   Interior of the Union Square Theatre. Note the steeply pitched Family Circle.
(Courtesy of the Billy Rose Theatre Collection, New York Public Library)

of the multi-talented Vokes Family from England in comic opera and burlesque. Despite Butler's efforts, and a successful seven-week run by the Vokes family, the theatre lost money.

Even while the Vokes family occupied the theatre, Shook had decided to transform the Union Square into a home for legitimate drama and was actively seeking a new manager. His eventual choice was Albert M. Palmer, a graduate of New York University School of Law and a librarian at the New York Mercantile Library. Palmer was a scholar and a devout theatre-goer, but had never worked in the theatre. The two men, however, shared the philosophy that "any play worth producing is worth producing in a manner approaching perfection as closely as human endeavor may hope to approach it," and Shook intuitively sensed qualities in Palmer that would suit him for management and would help lift the theatre out of an unsatisfactory financial condition.[21]

Butler retired from the theatre on June 1, 1872, and Palmer, at a salary of $25,000 a year, began as manager two days later. Until August, he was forced to present the variety acts that had been booked prior to his being hired; but with the departure of the Vokes family on August 10, Palmer closed the theatre for conversion from a variety house into a tasteful home for legitimate drama and set about creating a stock company to rival Wallack's and Daly's. "The first work of the carpenter's hammer was to dismantle the troughs in which the minstrels had washed their blackened faces" and Palmer's initial managerial act was to hire Dan H. Harkins from Augustin Daly's company as stage manager.[22]

Harkins informed Palmer that Agnes Ethel, Daly's leading lady, whose contract had expired, was seeking a manager to produce a play written for her by Victorien Sardou. With Harkins acting as intermediary, Palmer was introduced to Miss Ethel, signed the actress to a contract, and obtained the rights to present Sardou's *Andrea*. The manuscript, written in French, arrived just three weeks before the announced date of the opening, and after rapid and frantic translation, was put into rehearsal. Retitled *Agnes*, the play opened on September 17, 1872, with Ethel supported by Harkins, F. F. Mackay, Kate Holland, and Claude Burroughs. It was immediately successful, running 100 performances.

The success of *Agnes* shaped the career of the theatre. Melodrama became the standard fare at the Union Square, and Palmer finished assembling the company which would bring national fame to the theatre. The system of production adopted by the new company was a modification of the long-run: "while a new play was in constant preparation, the current offering was kept on the boards as long as the public demanded it, and old successes were revived from time to time."[23] This system afforded Palmer ample rehearsal time, during which the staging, acting and scenic elements were prepared and polished to the high degree traditionally associated with the Union Square company.

The Two Orphans, the production most frequently associated with the Union Square Theatre, and Palmer's greatest success, followed the pattern established by *Agnes*. The play, described as "a pathetic melodrama," opened on December

21, 1874, with Kate Claxton as the blind Louise. It was virtually unnoticed by the press and the *Times* carried a short, "routine" review, while there was no mention of the opening in either the *Tribune* or the *Herald*. By the fourth night, Christmas eve, first night patrons had evidently circulated favorable "word-of-mouth" reports and the theatre was filled to capacity. Thereafter, for the remainder of the 1874-75 season, *The Two Orphans* played to capacity houses, running for 180 consecutive performances and averaging $1,000 per night.[24]

For the next nine years, from 1874 to 1883, Palmer continued to feature the outstanding Union Square company in romantic melodramas, compiling a record of successes few other managers could match. In the seasons that followed *The Two Orphans*, *Rose Michel* with J. H. Stoddard as Pierre, *Miss Multon* (a French drama translated by A. R. Cazuran), *The Danicheffs* with James O'Neill, Charles Thorne, and Sara Jewett, *A Celebrated Case* starring Charles Coughlan as Jean Renaud and Agnes Booth as Madeline, and Bronson Howard's *The Banker's Daughter*, achieved fame at the Union Square, each running for more than 100 performances. *A Parisian Romance*, yet another melodrama translated from the French by Cazuran, served to introduce the then-unknown Richard Mansfield to New York audiences.

In 1883, Palmer temporarily retired from theatre management, traveled through Europe for a year, and returned to assume management of the Madison Square Theatre. Shook, in partnership with James W. Collier, continued to operate the Union Square Theatre for the 1884-85 season, presenting Palmer's former company, augmented by visiting stars, in plays such as *Stormbeaten*, *The Fatal Letter* by Cazuran, and Oscar Wilde's *Vera the Nihilist*. The first two plays were moderately successful, while the last was a dismal failure.

Shook ended his partnership with Collier in April 1885, disbanded the famous company, and leased the theatre to J. M. Hill, who had the reputation of being the most daring theatrical manager in the country. As manager of the Union Square, Hill continued his speculative habits. For his first production, Hill presented *Romeo and Juliet* with the then-unknown actress Margaret Mather as Juliet, even though the same play with the established Mary Anderson was just around the corner at the Star. The rival Juliets at the neighboring theatres quickly became a local topic of conversation and a frequent item in the press. Hill exploited the media coverage by clever advertising and by providing special excursion trains from the suburbs. Hill's shrewdness and nerve resulted in a run of 100 nights and established Mather as a star.

Hill opened the 1887-88 season with Stuart Robson and William H. Crane in Bronson Howard's *The Henrietta*, which continued for an uninterrupted run of 23 weeks. The play was scheduled to close on March 24, 1888, but late in the afternoon of February 28, the theatre and the hotel that housed it burned. Hill was in his office when a stagehand alerted him to the fire. On reaching the origin of the blaze, the cockloft above the auditorium, he found the entire loft and the top gallery in flames. While stagehands fought the fire in the cockloft, actors rushed to dressing rooms to gather their belongings; a large crowd, which included Henry Irving, who was appearing at the Star, gathered in the square (fig. 12). By the time the curtain was to have risen on the evening performance, the front of the Morton House, the theatre lobby, and the auditorium had been destroyed, but the stage suffered only water damage. Because of the vigilance and efficiency of the fire department, the Star was unharmed.

Late in the evening of the fire, Hill was at the Union Square Hotel publicly claiming that he would reopen the theatre within 30 days; but secretly he was already searching for a new house for the remainder of *The Henrietta* run. He not only failed to find a theatre for *The Henrietta*, but was forced to cancel the production of *The Possible Case*, which was scheduled to open in early April. The rebuilt Union Square, designed by John E. Terhune, with money provided by millionaire socialist Cortlandt Palmer, opened on March 28, 1889, with a production of *A Women's Stratagem*. For the next three years, Hill continued as manager without attaining the pre-fire level of success. He failed financially in 1892, and the lease was assumed by B. F. Keith and Edward Albee in May 1893 (fig. 13).

On September 18, 1893, the *Boston Herald* announced that "B. F. Keith's original idea, 'continuous performance,' had its New York introduction today and this evening, at Mr. Keith's Union Square Theatre. The house was packed from noon until the final curtain fell, and more delighted never sat in a New York theatre."[25] Actually, performances began at 12:30 and ended at 10:30, but the newspaper article is accurate on two critical points: Keith, a pioneer in big-time vaudeville, had expanded his operation to New York; and the concept of continuous performance, which was to revolutionize vaudeville, had likewise arrived in the city.

With continuous performances of "refined" vaudeville, Keith averaged in excess of $10,000 a week and temporarily brought new life to the dying Union Square area. In addition to continuous shows, Keith booked the best talent available (George M. Cohan first appeared as a "solo" act during the 1893-94 season) and consistently experimented with the latest innovations.

One of Keith's experiments was the introduction of movies into the bill. In 1894 the Holland brothers had opened a kinetoscope parlor at 1155 Broadway, which demonstrated the economic potential of movies; by late 1895, a virtual race had developed between several inventors to refine a machine that would project moving pictures on a screen. The race was won on April 23, 1896, when Thomas Edison publicly exhibited the Edison-Armat vitascope at Koster and Bial's Music Hall. Two months later, the *New York Times* carried the following announcement: "One of the several...equivalents of the vitascope, called the Lumière Cinématographe, will be placed on exhibition at Keith's Union Square Theatre" on June 29.[26]

Ironically, it was the fledgling movie industry that caused Keith to abandon vaudeville at the Union Square Theatre. Even at a 10-20-30^c scale, variety was unable to compete with the new movie houses in the Union Square area and Keith capitulated to the trend in 1908, converting the theatre into a film house called

Figure 12.   Burning of the Union Square Theatre and the Morton House. A portion of the crowd watching the fire is visible at the lower right-hand corner of the picture. *(Courtesy of the Hampden-Booth Theatre Library at The Players)*

Figure 13. The Portico of B. F. Keith's Union Square Theatre.
(Courtesy of the Theatre Collection, Museum of the City of New York)

the Bijou Dream. In 1914, B. F. Kahn assumed the lease and for the next eight years the theatre became part of Kahn's circuit of family burlesque theatres.

For the last 14 years of its existence, the theatre was a film house, known first as the Acme (1922-32), showing first-run films such as Mary Pickford's *Little Lord Fauntleroy* for 25ᶜ, and later (1932-36) as "the only American Soviet-Kino," presenting communist propaganda films. One of these, *The Man From the Restaurant*, presented a Marxian version of a Mary Pickford film. In 1936, the theatre was closed and the front lobby was demolished to make space for shops. A significant portion of the theatre from the dressing rooms and the balconies to the rear of the stage, however, was simply walled up and remains intact.[27] The roof and exterior shell are visible from the square and the side entrances can be viewed by peering through an iron gate on 4th Ave. just south of Union Square.

4

The Two Fourteenth Street Theatres

Between 1865 and 1868, two theatres that were to achieve fame in the remaining years of the nineteenth century were erected on opposite ends of 14th St. Both were called the Fourteenth Street Theatre, but there the similarity ended. The first, the Fourteenth Street Theatre at 105 W. 14th St., gained its reputation by presenting the luminaries of the legitimate stage while Tony Pastor's New Fourteenth Street Theatre at 141-43 E. 14th St. became immortalized as the birthplace of vaudeville.

The Fourteenth Street Theatre, located on the north side of 14th St. just west of 6th Ave., began its 72-year history as the Théâtre Français (fig. 14) on May 25, 1866. The building had been designed by Alexander Saeltzer, who had also planned the Academy of Music several blocks to the east, and was constructed between August 1865 and May 1866. According to several critics who attended the opening performance, the new theatre seemed like the old Academy "done in little," and its opening followed, ironically, by four days its famous ancestor's destruction by fire.

The façade of the theatre faced to the south and was of Philadelphia brick with freestone ornaments. Three sets of stairs with six steps each led from the street to five wide doors, the center three of which were flanked by lanterns fixed to the building. Above the doors, "five large windows, with arched heads shed light into the foyer on the second floor, and five smaller apertures" were placed above.[1] At the top of the façade, the name of the theatre was sculpted into a molded panel.

On leaving the street, the patron entered an outer vestibule, which was attractively frescoed and well lit, with woodwork and doors painted in French grey. Box offices were located on either side of the outer vestibule. Entry to the dress circle, second tier, and proscenium boxes was made through the three central doors, while the parquet was reached by the door on the right and the gallery by the one on the left. Once past the ticket takers, the patron passed through an inner lobby, decorated like the outer, and into a corridor that circled the auditorium which could accommodate 1,067 (fig. 15).

The parquet, composed of 362 maroon leather-covered armchairs from Paris (known as *Grands Confortables*), had a slightly concave floor and was 8 ft. below

Figure 14. The Théâtre Français.
(Courtesy of The New York Historical Society, New York City)

Figure 15. Interior of the Fourteenth Street Theatre After Some had Yelled "Fire."
(*Frank Leslie's Illustrated Newspaper*)

street level at its lowest point. A unique feature of the Théâtre Français was the relative absence of the iron pillars which, in most theatres of the era, obstructed spectators' view. Only eight columns were used in the new theatre and their diameter had been considerably reduced from the usual standard. These features, plus the fact that the *Grands Confortables* were roomier than conventional seats, made the parquet quite habitable.

Reviewing the opening night, the critic for the *Herald* alloted three columns to description of the auditorium, with half of a column devoted to the dress circle, which seated 230 patrons:

> The Dress Circle, destined to be the headquarters of the beau monde, comprises three rows of private boxes, the loges in the latter row being separated from each other by high partitions, which will prevent social intercourse . . . . The boxes in the Dress-Circle are handsomely carpeted and [adorned] with maroon damask. The gas-jets, en demi-cercle, shed lustre on the white and gold panellings of the balustrade attached to which are 18 Consols supporting gilded French eagles, each 24 inches in height.[2]

The second tier or balcony, provided with 180 *Grands Confortables* like those in the parquet, was decorated much as the dress circle. Imperial eagles were again in evidence and balustrades were adorned with gold and white panels. At the rear of the balcony, a mirrored lobby equipped with sofas and other furnishings provided a space for gatherings before the show or during intermissions. The third tier or gallery, which seated 175, provided high-backed benches at reasonable rates—75[c] for the reserved seats at the front and 30[c] for the remainder.[3]

The proscenium was decorated in gold and white and was flanked by statues of Apollo and of Bacchus riding a panther. The walls were painted in panels of gold and white with blue stripes and held globe lamps placed at suitable intervals. Maroon draperies, upholstery, and carpeting were employed throughout the house. Each balcony had railings and woodwork in gold and white and was furnished in front with a semicircle of globe lights. The total effect was generally felt to be simple and beautiful.

Throughout the theatre's history, people commented upon the ample stage and work space. *Julius Cahn's Official Theatrical Guide* lists the following dimensions for the stage: width of proscenium opening, 30 ft., 9 in.; height of proscenium opening, 30 ft.; footlights to back wall, 39 ft., 6 in.; curtain line to footlights, 2 ft.; distance between side walls, 72 ft., 4 in.; distance between fly girders, 47 ft., 2 in.; height from stage to rigging loft, 90 ft.; height from stage to working galleries, 23 ft. The theatre was equipped with sunken footlights, was provided with five sets of light ladders and boarders, and, according to Cahn, the "usual traps."[4]

For the theatre's opening on May 25, 1866, the first managers, M. Guignet and C. Drivet of Paris, selected *Nos Alliés,* a three-act comedy by Pol Mercier, and *Les Rendezvous Bourgeois,* an opera-bouffe in one act. The house was filled with New York's social elite and the opening was regarded as a grand success, but the average theatre patron evidently did not appreciate the offerings at the Théâtre Français. Attendance steadily declined, forcing Guignet and Drivet to abandon the theatre and return hastily to France, taking the statues of Apollo and Bacchus with them.

In August of 1866, Jacob Grau leased the house to present Adelaide Ristori (the first major star to appear at the theatre) as Medea in her American debut. Ristori remained at the theatre until the end of October, appearing in *Mary Stuart, Judith, Phaedra, Macbeth,* and *Elizabeth the Queen of England,* which had been written expressly for her by Paola Giacommetti.

In February 1871, William M. Holland rented the building, by then known as the Fourteenth Street Theatre, and presented Edwin Forrest in several of his greatest roles: *King Lear, Virginius,* and *Richelieu.* Forrest's appearance at the theatre marked his return to the stage after a three-year absence and, as it turned out, was to be the last of his career. The celebrated tragedian was 65 years old at the time and in failing health, a fact that sometimes created anxious moments for fellow actors and the theatre's manager. When Forrest failed to appear for the opening curtain one night, a near riot ensued.

Following Forrest's departure and a brief appearance in March by Marie Seebach, the noted German actress, Laura Keene leased the theatre, changed the name to Laura Keene's 14th Street Theatre, and opened in *Nobody's Child* on April 11, 1871. The production, however, failed to attract audiences and was replaced on April 17 by *Hunted Down.* This presentation also failed, closing after the first performance; Keene vacated the theatre the following day.

During the remaining months of 1871, the theatre changed hands several times and a major renovation was begun. Actor Charles Fechter purchased the property during the summer, borrowed money from Duncan, Sherman and Company, Bankers, and commissioned an extensive reconstruction of the building, which he renamed the Lyceum. The interior of the old theatre was torn out and totally remodeled, the façade was significantly changed (fig. 16) and "many novelties in the stage department were introduced."[5]

From the street, Fechter's new Lyceum Theatre looked entirely different from the original Théâtre Français. Over the three central doors Fechter constructed a portico supported by four pillars and graced on top by a decorative railing topped by four sets of globe lamps. The name of the theatre appeared on all three sides of the portico and globe lamps hung between the four front-most pillars. Small balconies, each supporting two sets of globe lamps, flanked the portico. Above, four pillars supported a panel on which the name of the theatre also appeared and a tympanum with a set of figures sculpted in bas relief. The third-story windows had disappeared in the reconstruction. At the top, a decorative railing like that on the portico enclosed the roof. The entire renovation cost a total of $250,000.

The grand opening of the Lyceum, featuring a performance of *The Count of Monte Cristo,* was scheduled for March 31, 1873, but it never took place. Duncan

Figure 16. The Fourteenth Street Theatre.
(Courtesy of the Theatre Collection, Museum of the City of New York)

and Sherman, displeased with Fechter's extravagance, legally seized the theatre, ousted Fechter's employees, and halted all work on the theatre, costing Fechter his entire investment, as well as that of a Miss LeClerq, a member of the company who had loaned Fechter money for renovations. On September 11, 1873, the theatre resumed operation under the management of William Mansell with a production of *The Hunchback of Notre Dame.*

In November 1876 James McVicker leased the theatre to present Edwin Booth in some of his best known roles, including *Hamlet, Richard the Third,* and *Othello.* The engagement ended on January 27, 1877, after two months. During the period of Booth's appearance, ticket speculation became a major problem for theatre managers throughout the city and theatre programs of that time (including the Lyceum's) contained warnings against such a practice. Also at this time, William Proctor established a bar in the basement of the theatre. During the closing years of the century, it became common knowledge that the bar was more financially successful than the box office and it was not an unknown occurrence for the company manager to borrow money from Proctor to pay the actors.

At the end of March 1879, J. H. Haverly, formerly of Chicago, assumed the lease to the theatre, changed the name to Haverly's Theatre, installed Haverly's Mastodon Minstrels and the Haverly Juvenile Opera Company on the renovated stage, and committed the theatre to the production of popular entertainments. Although Haverly occasionally presented Shakespeare, and Booth returned for a short engagement, local critics were set to wondering how they could "ever resuscitate the Lyceum Theatre" which, by 1880, had fallen "far below the hopes of its first owners," and rapidly was slipping into the second rank of New York theatres.[6]

During the 1880s and 1890s, under the management of J. W. Rosenquist, the theatre became a booking house known for its presentation of popular melodramas, an image that not even an appearance by the famed Modjeska in *Camille* could dispel.[7] By the close of the century, the Fourteenth Street's stage had seen such melodramas as *The Still Alarm,* which featured live horses and a fire engine; *Blue Jeans,* with the famous buzz-saw scene; *Darkest Russia;* a revival of *The Black Crook; The Great Diamond Robbery; East Lynn; The Octoroon;* and Denman Thompson's ever-popular, *The Old Homestead.* Rosenquist also booked Minnie Palmer and her Nude Statues, until the police developed a sudden interest in the theatre arts. In 1895, John Doris, who later would become proprietor of several dime museums in the city, sublet the theatre to present "continuous" vaudeville.

By the early years of the twentieth century, the theatre had been virtually forgotten by uptowners and had been reduced to presenting such fare as *Girls Will Be Girls,* featuring Al Leech and the Rosebuds (September 12, 1904). In 1911, the doors of the theatre closed and, with the exception of an occasional Italian play, remained closed until 1926.

In the early months of 1926, Eva LeGallienne, searching for a home for her newly formed company, discovered the "forgotten old playhouse where rats scampered familiarly through the dressing rooms and odors were both pungent and democratic."[8] Gaining possession of the theatre, however, proved to be a problem because the lease-holder, an Italian company, was reluctant to leave. Nevertheless, after lengthy negotiations, LeGallienne secured the lease and hurried renovations were undertaken in the summer of 1926. "The motheaten façade was encased in scaffolding on which painters worked feverishly, windows were mended, sagging doors reset."[9] On October 26, 1926, with a gleaming new sign identifying the building as the Civic Repertory Theatre and banners reading "Good Luck Civic Repertory" and "Welcome Eva LeGallienne" flying from adjoining buildings, Fourteenth Street once again became the home of quality drama.

For the next five years, the old building was to experience a renewed glory as *The Three Sisters, The Master Builder,* Susan Glaspell's *Interiors, Peter Pan, Camille,* and *The Would-Be Gentleman* were presented by Miss LeGallienne and her company. The new era, however, was not to last long. At the end of the 1930-31 season, Miss LeGallienne expressed a desire to take a year's leave from her managerial duties, vowing to return the following year with new ideas for subsequent seasons. She never did, and the Civic Repertory Theatre entered the pages of history.

After the Civic Repertory years, the theatre was used for a brief period by the newly formed Theatre Union, and Clifford Odets' *Waiting for Lefty* premiered there as a part of the Union's New Theatre Night. In the spring of 1936, another melodrama, *Bitter Stream,* was presented. It was the last live drama to be mounted at the theatre and in May 1938 the building was razed. During the late 1940s and the early 1950s the site was used first as a roller skating arena and then as a parking lot. At present, it is the location of Lynn's Department Store.

Four blocks to the east, at 141 E. 14th St., Tony Pastor's New Fourteenth Street Theatre was located in an "ungainly, red brick structure," Tammany Hall, the fourth home of the Tammany Society (fig. 17). The building, which was topped by the heroic figure of the Tammany Indian armed with tomahawk and scalping knife, was designed by Thomas R. Jackson and was officially dedicated on July 4, 1868. The new Tammany complex cost the taxpayers of New York $350,000.[10]

The hall, which Pastor made famous in the 1880s and 1890s as the birthplace of "clean" vaudeville (fig. 18), was one of several theatres located in the building. The Tammany Society, not requiring the entire structure for its own use, retained one room on the ground floor and rented out the remainder for entertainments. The hall that Pastor later converted into his famous theatre was rented to Dan Bryant's Minstrels, and the remainder of the building was leased for $25,000 per year to Henry C. Jarrett and Harry Palmer, who outfitted the rooms for amusements. On January 4, 1869, Jarrett and Palmer opened their space as a "variety palace, conceived in terms of the great London Music Halls."[11]

The ground floor of the Tammany amusement complex contained, in addition to the Tammany Society's room and Bryant's hall, a bar and several large open rooms "used as bazaars—where fancy articles of every description [were] on

Figure 17.   Tammany Hall and Tony Pastor's New Fourteenth Street Theatre.
(Courtesy of the Billy Rose Theatre Collection, New York Public Library)

Figure 18.   Entrance to Tony Pastor's New Fourteenth Street Theatre.
(*Courtesy of the Theatre Collection, Museum of the City of New York*)

sale."[12] The second floor of Jarrett and Palmer's variety palace was divided into another bar; a Ladies' Café where hot suppers, creams, and other delicacies were available; and a conversation salon, equipped with divans and fitted up in a "Turkish style." Jarrett and Palmer's main theatre, a two-level hall used for "principal performances," occupied the entire top floor. The basement contained an oyster saloon and a promenade hall where an orchestra played popular music, Punch and Judy shows were performed, and panoramas were occasionally presented. The Tammany variety palace was open from 7 p.m. to midnight each evening and the general admission of 50ᶜ admitted a patron to all of the attractions excluding Bryant's Minstrels.

The "main hall" on the third floor was a first-class theatre in all respects. The proscenium opening was 45 ft., the depth of the stage from the apron to the back wall was also 45 ft., and the width between the side walls was 100 ft. The auditorium consisted of a parquet, a parquet circle (dress circle), and 30 private boxes, all equipped with seats "similar to those used at Niblo's."[13] The main hall was inaugurated on January 4, 1869, with a performance that included a "ballet d'action" by Marie Bonfanti; a burlesque, titled "The Page's Revel, or A Summer Night's Bivouac"; a comic duet by Sheridan and Mack; a trapeze performance by the Victorellis; and an allegorical tableau, "The Birth of New York." The highlight of the evening was the singing of "The Star-Spangled Banner" by baritone Robert Green, accompanied by a boys' chorus.[14] Thereafter, "everything from grand opera to variety" was presented in the main hall.

On January 16, less than two weeks after the Tammany amusement complex was inaugurated, the 39- by 90-ft. promenade hall, which had been named the Café Amusant, opened in the basement. While the upstairs theatre occasionally offered "higher" forms of entertainment (classical concerts and opera), the Café Amusant was devoted solely to light entertainment: burlesques, tableaux, gymnastic exhibitions, pantomimes, and Punch and Judy shows. Throughout its short history, the Café maintained its own orchestra, a "corps de ballet" of 23 dancers, a pantomime troupe, and a two-man Punch and Judy company; it was reputed to be more popular with the patrons than the larger hall upstairs.[15]

Despite its initial success, the Tammany complex lasted only two seasons, closing as a regular place of amusement in June 1870. In its last two months, Josh Hart endeavored to save the Tammany, presenting London music hall style of entertainment, but with little success. Thereafter, only one or two rooms (Ferraro's Assembly rooms, devoted to concerts and lectures in the mid-seventies, and the hall later utilized by Pastor) were used for entertainments.

The same month that the Tammany complex closed, Dan Bryant abandoned his ground floor hall and moved to larger quarters uptown. For the next four years, the theatre was a booking house until Adolph Neuendorff assumed the lease in September 1874. Renamed the Germania Theatre, it became one of several houses in the neighborhood to present German drama. When Neuendorff's lease expired and his company vacated the theatre in May 1881, Pastor moved in and began redecorating in preparation for the first of many seasons he would present on 14th St.

Pastor's theatre (fig. 19) generally was regarded as too small to be a legitimate theatre, but it was well suited to variety. The house was 52 ft. square, could accommodate slightly more than 1,000 people, and featured a family circle, a parquet, a small orchestra pit, and two private boxes decorated with velvet and lace on each side of the stage.[16]

Unfortunately, this is the extent of the architectural detail available. A critic for the *Mirror* described the stage as spacious, but neither specific dimensions nor a description of stage equipment appeared in his review. Such information, usually printed in *Julius Cahn's Official Theatrical Guide,* was furnished for other variety houses, but, for some unknown reason, was omitted in the case of Pastor's theatre. The only graphic evidence of the theatre—exit diagrams in the programs—merely show that the auditorium was horseshoe shaped, indicate the position of the exits, confirm the number and location of the stage boxes, and reveal that there was access to the stage from one of the stage boxes.

When the theatre was rebuilt in 1888, following a fire that gutted the interior, the newspapers carried descriptions of the improvements. The basic plan of the theatre remained the same, but

> iron, brick and plaster had replaced wood throughout the house, and a new exit from the gallery had been provided. A new proscenium arch spanned the stage, supported on each end by two large columns and decorated in bas-relief with a center panel of Terpsichore flanked by medallions of Satire and Comedy. Patrons entered the lobby through a new portico with Corinthian columns, bevel-plate glass doors, and a colored glass transom. The walls of the lobby were now freshly plastered and floor tiled with white marble.[17]

The lobby also featured a new, brass-plated box office.

It is a common belief that vaudeville or "clean" variety was born the night Pastor opened his theatre on 14th St. The performance that evening, October 24, 1881, "was the first 'clean' vaudeville show and to its bill, as Fred Stone used to say, a child could take his parents."[18]

While it is debatable whether vaudeville was actually born on 14th St., as some scholars maintain, it certainly grew to maturity there.[19] With other first-class theatres in the vicinity, with the venerable Academy of Music as a next-door neighbor and Steinway Hall two doors to the west, with fashionable restaurants directly across the street, and major hotels nearby, the *haute monde* was attracted to the area. In addition, the area was far safer and more attractive to the ladies, who might have been hesitant to patronize Pastor's earlier Broadway theatre and most certainly would have avoided his former Bowery address. While Pastor's bills, house policies, advertising, and philosophy had changed little since his Bowery days, his New Fourteenth Street Theatre attracted more ladies and more middle- and upper-class patrons. As a result, variety gained an aura of respectability which heretofore it had lacked.

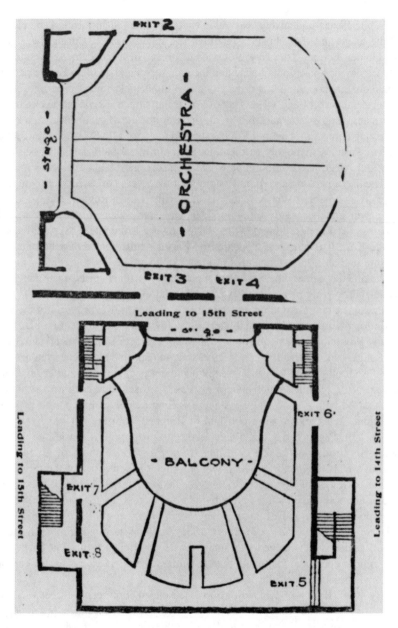

Figure 19. Diagram of Tony Pastor's New Fourteenth Street Theatre. *(Courtesy of the Billy Rose Theatre Collection, New York Public Library)*

While Pastor undeniably was aided by being in an ideal location, he clearly had the talent and show business acumen to capitalize on it. During the 1880s, his "Golden Period," the New Fourteenth Street Theatre became the model for early vaudeville houses nationwide and the area surrounding Union Square became his personal monopoly, a fact reflected in two of his nicknames: "The Impresario of Fourteenth Street" and "The King of Fourteenth Street." Rival managers, aware of his stature and aware that while in his theatres downtown he had shown a knack for driving competitors out of business, tended to avoid 14th St. when they moved uptown. Pastor's monopoly of the square remained virtually unchallenged until Keith and Albee leased the Union Square Theatre in 1893.

The list of performers whom Pastor either discovered or assisted early in their careers is a veritable "Who's Who" of vaudeville. Lillian Russell, Nat Goodwin, May Irwin and her sister Flo, Harrigan and Hart, Denman Thompson, Gus Williams, Pat Rooney, Maggie Cline (The Bowery Brünnhilde), Sophie Tucker, and the Kernell Brothers all appeared on Pastor's bills before they had attained stardom, and all acknowledged his influence on their careers. By 1885, aspirants to a vaudeville career knew that an appearance on the Fourteenth Street stage guaranteed booking in any other vaudeville house in the country.

Pastor's talent for finding and signing headliners, however, was not the only reason for his success. Each headliner was supported by 12 to 20 first-class acts (usually about 35 performers) and the bill was "characterized by speed and diversity. Songs, dances, acrobatics, mimicry, and dramatic and burlesque sketches succeeded each other without pause, keeping audiences entertained and eager to see the next act."[20] Unlike other managers, Pastor insisted that each act on his bill be rehearsed before appearing on stage to guarantee its quality. Those acts that had "gone stale" either were polished or dropped from the bill.

In 1879, Pastor had added a new feature to his programs: burlesque of light opera. His production of *T.P.S. Canal Boat Pinafore,* a spoof of Gilbert and Sullivan's *H.M.S. Pinafore,* which was the rage of New York at the time, was the first burlesque of light opera to be presented in a variety house. It was wildly popular and was copied immediately by other managers. Pastor himself continued to lampoon Gilbert and Sullivan with *The Pie-Rats of Penn Yann* (1881) and *Patience, or The Stage Struck Maidens* (1882).[21] While starring in *Pie-Rats,* Lillian Russell achieved full-fledged star status. Pastor continued to present burlesques of both light opera and legitimate theatre successes until 1886, when, for reasons unknown, he abandoned the form.

By 1890, Pastor's "Golden Period" had ended. Fourteenth Street was considered downtown and many of Pastor's previously faithful customers began deserting him to patronize Koster and Bial's and other uptown vaudeville houses. For a short time, Pastor, relying on old friends and foreign stars as headliners, fended off the challenge; but when Keith and Albee opened the nearby Union Square and adopted the continuous or "ferris wheel" show at prices of 15, 25, and 50^c, Pastor's two-a-day shows at the 20, 30, and 50^c scale, which he had maintained for years, were now in jeopardy. In 1896, Pastor and his longtime house manager, Harry Sanderson, announced that the traditional matinees (instituted while Pastor was at his Broadway theatre) would be eliminated, that three continuous shows would be presented daily, and that prices would be reduced. Clearly, by the mid-nineties the King of Fourteenth Street had lost control of his empire.

In the end, it was "the baby industry of motion pictures which robbed King Tony of his empire on Fourteenth Street."[22] In 1894, the Holland Brothers had opened a kinetoscope parlor at 1155 Broadway, and by the end of 1896, Koster and Bial's, Keith's Union Square Theatre, the Eden Musée on 23rd St., and Hammerstein's Olympia Music Hall were including movies on their bills. In 1899, Pastor himself added films to his programs.

By 1908 there were several movie houses within sight of Pastor's theatre. Responding to the changing conditions, Pastor signed a contract with William Rock of American Vitagraph in the spring of 1908 which detailed plans for converting his theatre into a movie house for the summer. According to the agreement, films would be shown until August and vaudeville would return in September. *Variety,* however, reported that Rock found competition with the other movie houses in the neighborhood so fierce that he withdrew from the agreement in July. Shortly after American Vitagraph abandoned the theatre, Pastor and Harry Sanderson announced that a new vaudeville season would begin as soon as entertainers could be signed.

The promised season, however, never materialized. Pastor had attempted, earlier in the year, to negotiate a year-to-year lease with the Tammany Society; the society, however, demanded a five-year lease. Too tired to move uptown and evidently frightened by Vitagraph's inability to compete with the movie houses in the vicinity, Pastor retired from show business. He died shortly thereafter. Sanderson, aware of the speed with which the city was growing and new buildings were being constructed, opened a real estate office and eventually became a millionaire.

After Pastor's death, the theatre was leased to Samuel Kraus and a Mr. Murray of the David Kraus Amusement Company, who changed the name to the Olympic Theatre and presented burlesque bills. The theatre continued operation as a burlesque house until it was demolished in 1928 as part of a plan to build a Consolidated Edison skyscraper on the land. Two years earlier, the other building on this plot, the venerable Academy of Music, had been razed for the same reason.

5

Concert-Lecture Halls

By the middle of the nineteenth century, concerts and lectures had become popular forms of entertainment in New York, often surpassing the opera and the theatre in total attendance. Musical concerts with the emphasis on opera, oratorios, or popular songs had been attracting audiences throughout the country since the mid-eighteenth century. Public lectures, growing from a self-education movement in the 1820s and popularized by the Lyceum circuit established in 1826, proliferated until the final years of the nineteenth century. By the time Union Square became the city's Rialto, lectures were so lucrative that managers were able to attract speakers of the stature of Charles Dickens, Mark Twain, Oscar Wilde, and Artemus Ward. Meanwhile, countless musicians flocked over from Europe to pick up substantial fees for performing at area concert halls.

Until the middle of the nineteenth century, New York's concert-lecture halls were located on Broadway and the Bowery south of 14th St.[1] Among the more popular were Castle Garden on the Battery, Niblo's Saloon at the northeast corner of Broadway and Prince St., and Tripler Hall at Broadway and Great Jones St. By the 1870s, however, concerts and lectures, like opera and the theatre, had followed the uptown movement, and concert-lecture halls dotted the area around Union Square. Many of these (Steck Hall, 11 E. 14th St.; Knabe Hall, 112 5th Ave.; and Weber Hall, 108 5th Ave.) were not actual theatres, but large chambers in the piano showrooms that abounded on 14th St. Commonly, these simple concert rooms featured a grand piano bearing "the maker's name on the side, in gilt Gothic letters about a foot high" at one end of the room and seated several hundred patrons in simple, portable wooden chairs.[2] Others, notably Steinway and Chickering halls, accommodated a more sizable audience in a theatre equipped with an elevated stage, a parquet and gallery, and loge seats bolted to the floor.

The first concert-lecture hall in the Union Square area opened in April 1854, six months before the Academy of Music. Dodworth Hall (also called Dodworth's Rooms or Dodworth's Saloon), located at 806-808 Broadway adjacent to Grace Church, had been opened as a dance academy in 1851 by Allen Dodworth, who advertised himself in the *New York City Directory* as "Professor of Music and Teacher of Dancing." A member of a family prominent in New York musical circles, Dodworth had established his first dance academy at 448 Broome St. in 1842 to teach "good manners and fine motion." In 1851, he moved to Broadway at 11th St., following the wealthy who constituted his clientele. He was promptly followed to the area by Ferraro's Dancing Academy (59 W. 14th St.) and M. Carrould, "instructor in the art of dancing" (54 E. 13th St.). In October 1854, Dodworth advertised that a new season of dance classes was about to begin and that his "elegant establishment [had] been additionally decorated and other improvements made during the summer."[3] One of the improvements in Dodworth's operation was the addition of concerts and lectures in his expanded facilities.

Dodworth's academy and his concert-lecture hall were situated in a four-story brownstone building just north of Grace Church (fig. 20). While it is known that Dodworth maintained dance studios on the second floor, virtually nothing is known about the location of the hall or its physical layout. Newspaper advertisements afford a record of the performers, but since the concerts and lectures presented were not reviewed, no description of the hall exists. Considering that there was no division of the seating into parquet and gallery in Dodworth's advertising, nor any mention of a stage in his announced renovations, it is likely that Dodworth Hall was simply a large room with portable chairs for spectators and a space left clear for the performers.

The hall was opened with a series of concerts by Aptommus, the harpist, in April and May 1854, and for the next four years was devoted almost exclusively to classical music. Between 1854 and 1858, Theodore Eisfeld's Classical Quartet was a regular fixture at Dodworth's Rooms; Maurice Gottschalk, the pianist, gave a "last" concert there; Sigismund Thalberg performed at several *Matinées Musicales;* Ole Bull played several "farewell" concerts; and Adelina Patti appeared on a program with other singers two years before her triumphant debut at the Academy of Music.

During the late 1850s and early 1860s, solo performers of the calibre of Ettore Brignoli and Agnes Sutherland, and groups such as the New York Harmonic Society and the Mason-Thomas Quartet, appeared regularly and Dodworth's Rooms became one of the city's most popular concert-lecture halls, eclipsing in reputation many of the downtown halls. During this period, Dodworth's was also becoming increasingly popular with the leading lecturers, elocutionists, and novelty performers. In January 1859, Fanny Kemble "gave intellectual delight reading . . . all the best-liked plays of the bard."[4] She was followed by George Vandenhoff, who narrated selections from Shakespeare, Dickens, and Sheridan. Later that spring, Adolph Neuendorff, then a vocal student of Dr. G. Schilling and later to become a prominent figure in the German theatre in the city, debuted at the hall, as did Little Ella who, at three and a half years of age, gave dramatic and poetic readings.

During the 1861-62 season, while the hall was at the height of its popularity, Dodworth moved his dance academy to a more fashionable location at 204 5th Ave. and 26th St., a building later occupied by Delmonico's. The hall retained the Dodworth name and was rented to various managers. Shortly after Dodworth

Figure 20.   Dodworth Hall.
   (Courtesy of The New York Historical Society, New York City)

moved uptown, it was leased to M. Guignet, later one of the initial managers of the Fourteenth Street Theatre, for a series of *Soirées Dramatiques* consisting of light vaudevilles, proverbs, and songs. From October to December 1861, the hall was occupied by Artemus Ward, one of the most original of American humorists, who gave a lecture-tour about life among the Mormons. Ward's lecture was accompanied by a piano (as were many lectures of the period) and employed a panorama of Mormon life which Ward estimated to contain over a mile of paintings.

In the mid-1860s, with the major musicians abandoning Dodworth's Saloon for the newer and more spacious Irving and Steinway Halls, Dodworth's maintained its position largely because of the appearances of some of the country's leading humorists. Ward returned several times during this period and the hall repeatedly hosted Alf Burnett, "Renowned Western Humorist, Eccentric Delineator, Exquisite Reciter, Great Facial Artist and Levitator," and humorist R. J. De Cordova, in sketches such as "Open Air Industry in New York," "The Puppy Dealer," "The Lung Tester," "The Telescope Man," and "The Self-sealing Envelope Man."[5] The hall's coffers were also greatly assisted in 1865 by a series of performances by Blind Tom, "sightless and untutored from birth—his very soul overflowing with musical genius."[6] Reputedly, he was the only pianist who could perform the secundo to any piece of music from memory.

By 1868, however, the prestige of the hall had declined and the following advertisement regularly appeared in the *Clipper:* "Dodworth Hall . . . to be let for concerts, balls, fairs or variety entertainments."[7] With few exceptions, however, concerts, balls, and fairs were given at the newer halls, leaving variety the most common fare at Dodworth's. Among the "regular" artists to appear there in the late 1860s were Professor Hartz, the magician; Signor Blitz, magician and ventriloquist; James Taylor, the English humorist; and the Georgia Minstrels. At times the hall was "metamorphized" into a house of wonders (a dime museum) featuring a two-headed girl, trained birds, and an exhibition of bullfrogs which, according to the ads, were almost as big as babies. Late in 1870, the hall was leased to Edwin Kelly of Kelly and Leon's Minstrels, who presented burlesques and sketches featuring "The Only Leon." By the 1871-72 season, Dodworth Hall had disappeared from *Rode's City Directory,* and only a few scattered, minor concerts were presented at the hall in the 1870s. In the 1880s the building became a furniture warehouse and it was torn down in 1887.

Irving Hall, one of the concert-lecture halls that contributed to the decline and eventual demise of Dodworth Hall, was constructed in 1860 for the express purpose of housing balls, lectures, concerts, and "miscellaneous entertainments of a high character." Situated at the southwest corner of Irving Place and 14th St., the two and one-half story building resembled a church more than it did a theatre (fig. 21). Wide stone steps led to three central doors which gave access to the hall. The hall itself (fig. 22) had no stage, but a flat floor with a small gallery. It possessed two private boxes and could accommodate more than a thousand spectators.[8]

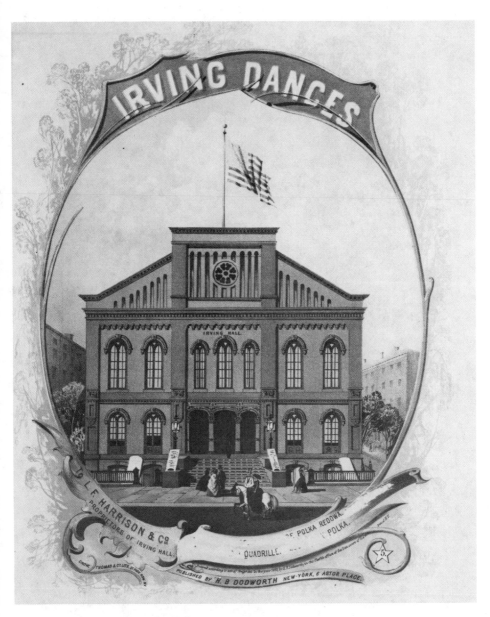

Figure 21. Irving Hall.
(*Courtesy of the Eno Collection, New York Public Library,
Astor, Lenox and Tilden Foundations*)

Figure 22. Interior of Irving Hall.
(Harper's Weekly)

The new hall was scheduled to open on December 18, 1860, with a concert featuring Pauline Colson, Adelaide Phillips, Ettore Brignoli, and Signor Susini. Several of the performers failed to arrive in the city on time, however, and the concert was postponed. Instead, the new hall had its maiden performance on December 20 when George Christy's Minstrels appeared for one night; the grand opening was held one week later, on December 27, with all of the scheduled artists present.

From the outset, Irving Hall was popular with theatre-goers. The Sunday Night Concert Series, inaugurated during the first season, was consistently well attended and the hall quickly became famous for its "pops" concerts given under the direction of Lafayette Harrison, an old-time impresario. Early in its history, Irving Hall also attracted many notable stars of the concert circuit: Maurice Gottschalk played a series of *matinées d'instrumentation* in an intimate in-the-round setting; Carl Formes, Brignoli, Susini, and other opera singers of the first rank appeared frequently; and the hall became temporary headquarters for both Theodore Eisfeld and the Philharmonic Society and Theodore Thomas' orchestra, considered by many to be the best in the city. The latter had the honor of introducing Schubert's *Unfinished Symphony* to American audiences in 1867.

In the early 1860s, Irving Hall was graced by regular appearances by Carlotta Patti, Adelina's sister, who after her debut at Dodworth Hall on October 25, 1860, rapidly became a favorite of the concert stage. Possessing a beautiful voice and an "exquisite style," Carlotta unfortunately was confined to the concert stage by a lameness that made the rigors of opera impossible for her. "But for the disability just mentioned, she would doubtless have had a brilliant career in opera."[9]

Beginning in 1863, miscellaneous entertainments, not necessarily of the "highest character," shared the stage with concerts. In March 1863, General and Mrs. Tom Thumb exhibited themselves in their wedding apparel to thousands of curious spectators, guaranteeing a substantial profit for Irving Hall's board of directors. Three months later, the hall was the site of a billiard match between Dudley Kavanaugh, William Goldthwait, Philip Tieman, Victor Estephe, Louis Fox, and other top players from around the country. The match, sponsored by Chris O'Conner's Billiard Saloon on East 14th St., offered a $1,000 prize to the winner. After 10 days, Kavanaugh claimed the prize. From late June to October of the same year, Fallon's Stereopticon of Foreign Scenes attracted large audiences to the hall.[10] The stereopticon was described as

photography of extraordinary dimensions, of 25 feet in diameter, or covering six hundred square feet of surface, brilliantly illuminated bringing into distinct relief the most delicate and minute details of the photograph, and accompanied with such stereoscopic effects as to be absolutely startling in illusion.[11]

The seasons between 1864 and 1866 proved to be the best in the hall's 28-year history. Theodore Thomas continued to use the hall; Mme Parepa-Rosa made her American debut there on September 11, 1866; both De Cordova and Artemus Ward lectured frequently; Blind Tom played a series of concerts for three weeks; and the unveiling of a new type of organ built by J. H. and C. C. Odell took place in April 1866. During this period, the hall also housed its share of novelty and variety shows, with Hartz the Magician renting the hall in September 1866 and Oscanyan's Gynecocracy or *Soirées Orientales* occupying the main floor for two weeks in October.[12] These consisted of lectures on Turkey accompanied by "living illustrations," Turkish music, singing, and dancing. After May 1866, Irving Hall was booked continuously as performers, originally scheduled to appear at the recently burned Academy of Music, moved across Irving Place.

The fortunes of Irving Hall, at their zenith in the spring of 1866, plummeted quickly after the opening of neighboring Steinway Hall in October of the same year. Many of the Irving Hall stalwarts, including the Thomas orchestra, the Philharmonic Society, and the Sunday Night Concerts, deserted the older hall, eager to perform at the newer, larger, and better publicized theatre around the corner. Within two years, concerts and lectures were rare occurrences at Irving Hall and the space was rented mainly for variety and for balls. Because of its large floor with ample viewing space in the galleries and the tunnel connecting it to the Academy of Music, the hall remained one of the city's more popular ballrooms until its demolition in 1888.

During the late 1860s and early 1870s, Irving Hall became a popular spot for visual shows. In 1868, Fallon's Stereopticon was once again installed in the hall, as was Kinney's Moving Diorama of Lincoln's Funeral. A year later, the hall housed a "Germania," a moving panorama of the Franco-Prussian war with vocal accompaniment by Karl Formes, W. J. Hill, and Sarah Barron. With entertainments of this sort plus the usual number of balls, Irving Hall was able to limp along until 1877, when it became a variety house, first called the Irving Music Hall and then the Grand Central Theatre. The Grand Central, managed by John Wild, opened as a "First Class Society Vaudeville Theatre" on November 28, 1877, with a bill featuring Mlle Frochard's Female Minstrels and Rollin Howard's Burlesque Troupe.[13] The following week, the bill contained Si Slocum's Female Bathers, 100 specialty artists of various sorts, and 50 ladies in a single minstrel scene.

By June 1878, Wild and his "Society Vaudeville" had abandoned the hall, which resumed its original name. During the early summer, Edison demonstrated his newly invented phonograph with well-known musicians such as Jules Levy, the cornetist, participating. The invention was able to reproduce the sound of Levy's cornet but, with its tinny sound, it failed to impress the public. After this, the hall fell into disuse, with advertisements for performances rarely appearing in the daily newspapers. It was demolished in July 1888 and the Amberg Theatre (later the Irving Place Theatre) was promptly erected on the site and opened in December of 1888.[14]

In 1866, Steinway Hall, one of the most famous concert rooms in New York City musical history, was opened at the rear of the Steinway and Sons' piano showroom at 71-73 E. 14th St. (between Union Square and Irving Place). The hall was the creation of William Steinway, whom Robert Grau credits with doing "more for musical progress and [doing] it less ostentatiously than any American . . . history can recall."[15] Steinway's interest in promoting musical endeavors was evidenced not only by his sponsoring many musicians of international stature, but by the fact that his famous hall was always available rent free to performers who offered entertainment which was both "artistic and educational."

The hall (fig. 23), constructed entirely of white marble, stood four stories high and extended to 15th St. Wide, single doors on both 14th and 15th streets afforded access to the concert hall and opened outward to provide a rapid means of escape in the event of fire.

Upon entering the ground floor of the building from 14th St., the patron first passed through a small concert room used for musical events that required an intimate setting. At the far end of this room, which held 400 spectators, a sliding partition opened directly into the rear of the main hall. For major events, such as orchestral concerts, the two halves of the partition were slid to the side, creating one large theatre.

With the partitions open, the hall could accommodate 3,000 spectators (fig. 24); 1,300 on the ground floor (parquet), 800 in the two balconies, 400 in the "extension room," and 500 standing. Seats in the parquet and balconies were permanently attached iron-framed arm chairs, cushioned with red leather. With unusually wide aisles and ample space between rows, there was general agreement that Steinway Hall was exceptionally comfortable.

Steinway Hall differed from Dodworth and Irving Halls not only in size, but in its being equipped with a permanent stage (fig. 25). Ornately decorated with busts, statues in recessed niches, sets of gas lamps on the walls, and carved moldings and small balconies over the entrances at each side of the stage, it closely resembled European concert halls. The most famous feature of the stage was the built-in pipe organ which was reputed to have been one of the largest and best in the world when it was installed.

The new hall was dedicated on October 31, 1866, with a concert that befitted its stature in the musical world. The premiere featured the H. L. Bateman company, which included Mme Parepa-Rosa, Carl Rosa, and Signors Brignoli, Ferranti, and Fortuna, accompanied by the Theodore Thomas orchestra. Highlights of the concert included "Bel Raggio" from *Semiramide* and "The Nightingale's Trill" both sung by Parepa, and "Da quel di" from *Linda de Chamounix,* rendered by Parepa-Rosa and Brignoli.

The elite of both the concert and lecture worlds were quick to follow. Adelaide Ristori, the Italian tragedienne, read from the Italian poets on November 13; De Cordova brought his humorous sketches, including "That Dog Next Door" and

Figure 23. Steinway Hall.
  (*Courtesy of the Theatre Collection, Museum of the City of New York*)

Figure 24.   Interior of Steinway Hall.
(*Lansing's Pictorial Diagrams of the Leading Opera*
Houses, Theatres, etc. in the United States)

Figure 25.   Theodore Thomas and His Orchestra on the Stage of Steinway Hall.
(Courtesy of The New York Historical Society, New York City)

"The Great Divorce Case" to Steinway in December of 1867; Fanny Kemble read from Shakespeare the following March; Paul du Chaillu gave his popular lecture on the gorilla the same month; and he was followed by Ole Bull. The major event of 1867 on the lecture platforms of the city, the appearance of Charles Dickens, also was held at Steinway Hall beginning on December 9. Dickens continued at the hall until the end of December, reading from his Christmas sketches, the *Pickwick Papers, Nicholas Nickelby,* and other works to the delight of both the critics and the public. The critic for the *Tribune* raved:

> Mr. Dickens is not only an excellent reader but a greatly-gifted actor . . . . In reading as well as writing he enters into every character that he creates. Now he is Scrooge, presently he is Mr. Fezziwig, anon he is Bob Cratchit.[16]

By 1870, Steinway Hall was undisputedly the leading concert-lecture hall in the city. The Theodore Thomas orchestra, the Philharmonic Society, and the Oratorio Society made it their regular home; both Adelina and Carlotta Patti sang concerts there; and Christine Nilsson made her American concert debut at Steinway Hall on March 14, 1870. Two years later, William Steinway, in conjunction with manager Jacob Grau, scored the musical "coup" of the season, presenting Anton Rubinstein, the legendary Russian pianist, and Henri Wieniawski, acclaimed the greatest of living violinists. The "Russian cohorts" quickly became the rage in New York; before they ended their tour, they had presented more than 50 concerts, the last being held at Steinway Hall.

The lecturers at Steinway Hall during the 1870s were equally renowned. Edwin Booth read poetry to musical accompaniment (February 1870), Edwin Forrest read from Shakespeare (November 1871), Charlotte Cushman presented a series of readings in February 1874, and Mrs. Scott-Siddons read from the Bard and other poets in 1879. Steinway Hall also remained popular with the humorists. De Cordova returned regularly and, in January 1872, Mark Twain appeared at the hall for one night, presenting a sketch entitled "The Man Who Laughs."

Throughout its illustrious history, Steinway Hall remained a "high-class" auditorium with popular entertainments appearing infrequently and generally relegated to secondary importance. Variety and novelty acts did, nevertheless, play there from time to time. During the 1874-75 season, Fred McCabe presented "a Vocal, Ventriloquial, Musical, and Sartorial Melange in which he [displayed] his marvelous power of Changing the Voice, Figure and Face, with Rapid Changes of Picturesque Costume."[17] In 1877, the hall hosted The Great National Baby Show, and later the same year Maurice Strakosch inaugurated the popular and famous Telephone Concerts in which an instrument, usually a piano, played in Philadelphia or some other distant city was heard on the Steinway Hall stage. Later these concerts were refined so that a violinist in Steinway Hall would play a selection accompanied by a pianist in another city. In July of the following year,

Edison's Speaking Phonograph was shown and the same exhibition that had failed at Irving Hall the month before was an immediate success at Steinway Hall.

Unlike Dodworth and Irving Halls, which faded rapidly from prominence once newer halls were built, Steinway Hall declined gradually and the auditorium was never forced to revert to "cheaper" forms of entertainment in its later years. During the 1880s, it continued to attract first-class concert artists, including the teenage Fritz Kreisler in his American debut, and an appearance by Victor Herbert, "fresh from the court of Würtemberg, where he was violinist to the king."[18] The Theodore Thomas concerts continued to attract large and refined audiences and the Young People's concerts were as good as they were when they began. In 1890, two years before Carnegie Hall opened, the large auditorium formally was closed. The smaller chamber-room remained open and was used until 1926, when Steinway and Sons abandoned the building to move to their present quarters on West 57th St. The original Steinway Hall was replaced by a six-story loft building which currently occupies the site.

As famous as Steinway Hall, Chickering Hall, home of the Mendelssohn Glee Club, opened in 1875 at 130 5th Ave., on the northwest corner of 5th Ave. and 18th St. The new hall replaced the smaller Chickering Rooms at Broadway and 4th St. and immediately became popular with the New York concert audience which, by 1875, was large enough to support two first-class concert-lecture halls. Like Steinway Hall, Chickering Hall resembled a small theatre, with a stage, a parquet, and a gallery. Likewise, it was constructed by a prominent piano manufacturer as a combination showroom and concert-lecture hall.

The hall, built on the site of the former Sidney Mason residence, was designed by architect George B. Post and was constructed entirely of red stone (fig. 26). It occupied approximately half of the block lot between 18th and 19th streets, and was eight stories tall to the tip of the ventilating cupola perched atop the steeply pitched roof. Entrance to both the hall and the showrooms was through a mammoth set of doors on 5th Ave.

The concert hall itself was divided into a parquet and a balcony, both equipped with permanently attached chairs (fig. 27). Seating capacity was 1,300, with room at the rear of the hall for several hundred standees. The stage was 61 ft. wide by 28 ft. deep with a curved apron for the conductor or featured performer and was constructed without a proscenium arch. Like Steinway Hall, Chickering Hall was equipped with a pipe organ built into the walls on both sides of the stage.

From its opening, Chickering Hall was seldom unoccupied and consistently was listed in the newspapers among New York's first-class entertainment spots. Unlike Steinway Hall, which was known primarily for its high-class concerts and lectures, "a wide variety of entertainment appeared [at Chickering Hall] throughout the years, a jumble of events for many tastes."[19] This jumble included, in addition to more conventional variety entertainments, séances and other demonstrations of spiritualism, tableaux vivants, a women's suffrage convention, and a contest be-

Figure 26.   Chickering Hall.
(Courtesy of The New York Historical Society, New York City)

Figure 27. Interior of Chickering Hall.
(Lansing's *Pictorial Diagrams of the Leading Opera
Houses, Theatres, etc. in the United States*)

tween artists to determine who could draw the fastest. For this last event, "easels were set up on the stage to serve Napoleon Sarony, E. W. Kemble and other artists who drew pictures for an eagerly interested audience."[20]

Befitting a major concert-lecture hall, Chickering Hall was dedicated with a concert by a leading classical artist, pianist Hans von Bülow. It also became the New York home of two major musical organizations, the Mendelssohn Glee Club, directed by Edward McDowell, and the Boston Symphony Society. Thereafter, throughout its 18-year history, the hall continued to attract the best singers and instrumentalists, including Franz Liszt, Rubinstein, Paderewski, Brignoli, Carlotta Patti, and soprano Henrietta Beebe.

If Chickering Hall was well known for concerts, it was even more famous for its lectures. In its first years, George Vandenhoff and De Cordova found the new hall ideal for their presentations, and Victoria Clafin Woodhull, who had gained a measure of notoriety as a spiritualist and a leader in the suffrage movement, delivered a lecture entitled "A Prophetic Vision of the Future." Miss Woodhull's visit on November 21, 1876, followed by a month two lectures, "The Ministry of Wealth" and "Hard Times" by Henry Ward Beecher, pastor of Plymouth Church, Brooklyn, and one of America's most famous preachers.

The most celebrated series of lectures ever presented at Chickering Hall took place in January 1882 when the infamous Oscar Wilde made his American debut as a reader. For the initial lecture on January 10, 1882,

all New York was there. At five o'clock no more tickets were to be had. Even the speculators had but a few left . . . . Inside, the hall was packed. There was not room left for another spectator . . . . At 8:30 Mr. Wilde appeared. He was strikingly dressed in a regulation swallow-tail coat with white satin low cut vest, double buttoned; black knee-breeches, black silk stockings and low-cut shoes. A single diamond stone in the exact center of his expansive shirt front, and a fine handkerchief was thrust negligently between it and his waistcoat.[21]

Wilde's debut was a resounding success, doing much to dispel the popular notion that he was a "posturing idiot," and it guaranteed capacity houses for the remainder of his stay in America.

In addition to serving as a platform for lectures on "worthy" subjects, Chickering Hall also gained a certain measure of notoriety from the novelty and variety entertainments presented there. Programs of the times testify to the presentation of "Artistic Views, Exhibited by the Oxy-Hydrogen Light," "Cosmographic Illustrations of the Growth of Civilisation, the Rise and Decline of Art, and the Monuments of Human History," and burlesque temperance lectures, as well as the first interstate telephone call in history.[22] The call was made on May 17, 1877, from New Brunswick, New Jersey, 32 miles from New York, to Alexander Graham Bell, seated on the Chickering Hall stage and was witnessed by a packed house.

Old programs also document the appearance of more conventional variety performers. In the hall's second season, General Mite and Lucia Zarate, the famous midgets, were on view to curious New Yorkers, and Slavin's Minstrels presented a benefit later in the same season. The hall also was used on occasion for amateur minstrel nights which emphasized impersonations and sight gags, practically eliminating singing and dancing from the bill. In 1880, audiences were treated to genuine slave songs by the Jubilee Singers, a group composed of former slaves, singing the spirituals they had sung while still in bondage.[23] During Chickering Hall's existence, many of vaudeville's premiere performers, including Tony Pastor, Gus Williams, Lillian Russell, and the Irwin Sisters, also played there.

In 1893, Chickering Hall, like Steinway Hall before it, fell victim to the uptown movement of the entertainment industry. With audiences diminishing, the Chickering Company decided to close the hall and convert the space into a warehouse. Later in the same year, the property was sold, the hall demolished, and an office building constructed on the site.

6

Early Popular Entertainments in the Union Square Area, 1851-1870

During the late 1840s, when Union Square was still one of the city's most exclusive residential areas, popular entertainments were located primarily on Broadway and the Bowery below 8th St. At Barnum's Museum on the corner of Broadway and Ann St., the curious could view a practically unlimited selection of oddities, attend moral lectures, or witness the skills of jugglers, sword swallowers, trained animals, magicians, and ventriloquists, all for 25ᶜ. Those New Yorkers who were eager to escape the chaos of city streets could find both refuge and entertainment at either Vauxhall Pleasure Garden (on the Bowery between 4th and 8th streets) or at Niblo's Garden (at Broadway and Prince St.), where the entertainment ranged from drama to lectures to minstrel shows.

Circuses also flourished in the 1840s, utilizing any space large enough to house their operations. In one year alone, 1848, three major circuses were attracting large audiences: the New Broadway Circus, starring English riding master Harry Whitby and American clown Alexander Rockwell, occupied the Alhambra near Spring St.; the Sands, Lent and Company Circus pitched a huge tent, holding 5,000 spectators, at 8th St. near the Astor Place Opera House; and Van Amburgh's Circus entertained at the Zoological Hall, 35-37 Bowery.[1]

Those interested in panoramas, which were becoming the rage in the 1840s, could view countless yards of painted canvas. Brunetti's Panorama of Jerusalem was on view at 598 Broadway; Banvard's giant panorama of the Mississippi, featuring three miles of canvas, occupied the Panorama Building adjoining Niblo's Garden; Harrington's Sacred Diorama of the Creation of the World and the Deluge was at 396 Broadway above Stoppani's Baths; and Barnum's Museum housed several different panoramas during the decade. By the beginning of the next decade, the panorama had moved to within a block of Union Square, becoming the first popular entertainment form to invade the future Rialto. Satler's Panoramas (also advertised as Satler's Cosmoramas and Satler's Dioramas) opened in 1851 at Broadway and 13th St. and continued operation until 1853.[2]

In the late 1850s, vacant lots near the square were occasionally converted into circus grounds for the summer months. On June 1, 1859, Harry Whitby and Company's Circus pitched its tent in a lot at the southwest corner of 6th Ave. and 15th St. Five days later, Joe Pentland's Circus, started several years earlier by Pentland, a well-known clown of the era, began a summer of performances at Broadway and 13th St. In a building at 39 Union Square, a circus of a different sort was presented: Signor Bertolotto's exhibition of educated fleas. Bertolotto's flea circus featured diminutive "performers" dancing a polka, drawing miniature carriages and street cars, and impersonating Don Quixote and Sancho Panza. The following year, P. T. Barnum and James M. Nixon, an established ringmaster and circus entrepreneur, created an exhibition called The California Menagerie on the lot occupied the previous year by Pentland. The exhibition featured a collection of wild beasts and trained animal acts with J. C. Adams, "the California Trapper of '49," putting the animals through their routines. Each circus played for only one season near Union Square and then moved to another location in the city.

The first resort near Union Square devoted exclusively to popular entertainments to achieve any recognition or longevity was a pleasure garden, the Palace Garden, at the northwest corner of 6th Ave. and 14th St. (fig. 28). The garden was opened in 1858 by Cornelius V. Deforest and a partner known simply as Mr. Tisdale on a 200 by 300 ft. plot leased from the heirs of John Tonnele, a prominent merchant during the 1820s and '30s.[3] When Deforest and Tisdale established their pleasure garden, the original Tonnele home near 6th Ave. and 15th St. was converted into a restaurant called the Mansion House.

As depicted in written descriptions and an 1856 lithograph by the firm of Sarony, Major and Knapp, the Palace Garden included a two-level octagonal pagoda for orchestras, a platform for staging fireworks displays, a large fountain that doubled as a fish pond, and a 100 by 75 ft. tent used as a salon. Throughout the garden, "serpentine gravel walks . . . passed under elaborate cast-iron arches enriched with colored-globe gas lamps. Along the walks and throughout the grounds [were] placed 'statues of heros or heroines of mythology and modern times' and transparent or illuminated 'scenic pedestals' done in stained glass."[4]

When the Palace Garden opened on July 1, 1858, Deforest and Tisdale hoped that it would become "the resort of the refined, fashionable and the intellectual," and their evening *promenade concerts d'eté* were made up of instrumental selections designed to appeal to upper-class patrons. The garden's regular orchestra, conducted by Thomas Baker, was supplemented by Harvey Dodworth's Band, Wallace's Brass Band, and Robertson's Military Band. The highlight of the first summer was the appearance of Carl Formes, a favorite of New York opera fans.

During the first season, however, it became apparent that the Palace Garden was not destined to be a resort attended exclusively by the upper classes. The garden became a favorite gathering place during the day for housemaids and their infant charges and attracted the working classes from other parts of the city in such large numbers that "by the neighbors it was looked upon as the one blemish in [an] otherwise impeccable habitation."[5] Sensitive to the wishes of their clientele, Deforest and Tisdale dutifully provided children's matinees which included ventriloquism,

Figure 28. Lithograph of the Palace Garden.
(Courtesy of The New York Historical Society, New York City)

magic, and Indian dances. At the same time, they publicly announced that the "masses" were welcome and that the Palace Garden would provide "cheap entertainment" for their enjoyment.[6]

Deforest and Tisdale increased their appeal to the working classes not by replacing the promenade concerts, but by augmenting them with proven variety acts, many regarded as traditional fare for pleasure gardens. Routinely, fireworks displays, balloon ascensions, magicians, and "authentic" exhibitions of Indian life were presented on the same program with waltzes, quadrilles, and galops. In their first season, the proprietors also offered free gifts to the ladies who patronized the garden, a gimmick commonly attributed to Tony Pastor. In a departure from its London counterparts and earlier New York gardens, the management of the Palace Garden steadfastly refused to serve liquor on the grounds.

At the end of the first summer, Deforest and Tisdale, evidently encouraged by the season's profits, erected an amphitheatre with wooden sides and a canvas top that covered the portion of the garden abutting 6th Ave. The new amphitheatre accommodated 1,600 spectators, contained a center ring or "equestria" roughly 30 ft. in diameter, was lit by "an enormous chandelier suspended over the center of the ring, and . . . was heated by steam pipes run beneath the seats."[7] With its "equestria" and steam heat, the building quickly became popular with local circus managers looking for a winter home. In the first few months of its existence, the amphitheatre housed Pentland's, Whitby's, J. Van Amburgh's, and Nixon and Kemp's circuses, as well as Professor Starr's Menagerie and Side Show.

In the winter of the following year, Deforest, then sole proprietor of the Palace Garden, made additional improvements on the property. He razed the amphitheatre and salon and erected a permanent structure which measured 50 by 200 ft. The new hall, dubbed the Palace Garden Music Hall, was located on the western border of the property and could comfortably seat 3,000. While the construction of the new hall did little to elevate the class level of his patrons, it did allow Deforest to continue concerts during the winter. In 1860, the hall was redecorated with a profusion of flowers, trees and shubbery and at the same time a new salon and an aviary were added.[8]

In July of 1861, James M. Nixon assumed management of the garden, with Colonel T. Allston Brown serving as his business manager. Baker's orchestra was retained and the garden continued to present concerts, but Nixon added pantomime to his programs and permanently installed Nixon's Royal Circus and Menagerie of Living Animals in one of the pavilions. Since Nixon planned to pattern his operation after London's Cremorne Gardens, he changed the name of his establishment to Nixon's Cremorne Gardens.

During his first winter as proprietor, Nixon undertook a massive renovation of the grounds and buildings. The Music Hall was transformed into a 2,000-seat theatre called the Palace of Music, complete with "a spacious and handsome stage, new scenery, curtains, proscenium, chandeliers," and a balcony at the rear of the auditorium.[9] The salon was converted into the Hall of Flora, which was attached to a new 2,000-seat amphitheatre for equestrian exhibits. The renovation also included a complete restructuring of the grounds and erection of a second pagoda for orchestras.

The level of entertainment during Nixon's first full season as manager (the summer of 1862) matched the grand scale of the renovated garden. Pantomimes, added the previous season, were increased in importance, and Commodore Foote and Colonel Small appeared in the garden, riding in a beautiful chariot, drawn by Lilliputian ponies. Susini, Carlotta Patti, and Isabella Cubas gave concerts, Campbell's Minstrels and Buckley's Serenaders entertained, and clowns Tony Pastor, William Lake, Signor Blitz, and W. Donaldson (billed as the black clown and a former member of Charles White's Serenaders) regaled the crowds with their antics. Especially enticing to pleasure-seeking New Yorkers was a 25ᶜ admission ticket, which entitled the patron to partake of all of the attractions and entertainments the garden offered.

For reasons never made public, Nixon did not open the garden in 1863. Most likely, he realized that it was impossible to operate the garden at a profit on the scale he had envisioned and decided to avoid future losses. In 1864, a portion of the garden was used for the Sanitary Commission Fair and the following year the plot became the site of the Fourteenth Street Theatre.

Nixon did not remain out of business for long after closing his Cremorne Gardens on January 3, 1863. By August of the same year, he had erected a modest amphitheatre with wooden sides and a canvas top, called Nixon's Alhambra, directly across 14th St. from the Academy of Music. From August to the onset of cold weather in October, Nixon presented equestrian shows, charging 25ᶜ admission to the pit and 50ᶜ for the dress circle.

By February 1864, Nixon had replaced the temporary Alhambra with a larger permanent structure, the Hippotheatron, which was heated by steam and usable throughout the entire year. The circular building (fig. 29) was modeled after a Paris amphitheatre called the Champs Elysées and was constructed entirely of corrugated iron. The roof was surmounted by a cupola from which flew a large flag containing the figure of a horse, and the arched main entrance was adorned with globe lamps and statuary. Oversized American flags flew from flagpoles on either side of the building and posters on 14th St. advertised the evening's attractions.

Inside, "the main supports of the dome were a series of columns" encased in corrugated iron and graced with statues mounted on pedestals (fig. 30).[10] Seating was divided into three distinct sections: nearest the ring, the orchestra accommodated 600 spectators in seats costing 75ᶜ; above that, the dress circle seated 500 people and cost 50ᶜ; and the topmost section of the auditorium, mysteriously labeled the "pit" at the Hippotheatron, had a capacity of 600, each seat costing 25ᶜ. Above the seats, a wide carpeted promenade circled the entire building, providing standing room for 600 more spectators and increasing the total capacity of the house

Figure 29. The Hippotheatron.
(Courtesy of the Theatre Collection, Museum of the City of New York)

to 2,300. "The distance from the ring curb to the topmost seat was 22 ft. and, as each seat rose tier by tier, in an unbroken circle, every spectator had an excellent view of everything that was going on."[11]

The ring at the Hippotheatron, measuring 43 ft. 6 in. was reputedly the largest in any permanent structure in the United States, and larger than the rings at Astley's in London and the Cirque Napoléon in Paris. Two wide entrances exactly opposite each other provided access to the ring and constituted an improvement over previous amphitheatres, especially for spectacular pieces and for daring leaps.

Billed as a "new and superb equestrian temple" and "the model amphitheatre of the world," the Hippotheatron opened to the public on February 8, 1864, with an equestrian show that also featured the comic talents of Nat Austin and James Cooke. In April, Nixon, who now advertised himself as director of amusements, brought Eaton Stone, one of the country's premiere equestrians, to the Hippotheatron. The establishment was now well on its way to becoming one of New York's favorite amusement spots.

In addition to equestrian feats and acrobatics, Nixon included the pantomimes that had proven popular at his Cremorne Gardens, relabeling them "Harlequinades." The bill for December 26, 1864, was typical of the shows Nixon presented. It opened with an overture conducted by H. Wayrauch, the Hippotheatron's musical director, followed by the *Grande Entrée* on horseback of the entire company, billed as Knights and Ladies of Palestine. There followed a comic musical act, a double act on horseback performed by Master and Miss Stickney entitled "Posturing Wonderful," and an educated monkey. The last two spots on the first part of the bill were filled by the headliners, equestrians Robert Stickney and "mad" Louise Tourniaire. The second portion was devoted to *The Harlequin Blue Beard*, a "Comical, Oratorical, Farcical, Diabolical, Allegorical CHRISTMAS PANTOMIME."[12]

In 1865, history repeated itself as Nixon failed to reopen his new establishment for a second season. The Hippotheatron was bought by Dick Platt and rented to Lewis B. Lent, who changed the name to Lent's New York Circus. Nat Austin was hired as director of amusements and in the company was Fred Levantine of the Levantine Brothers, equilibrists, who later gained show business fame as the vaudeville impresario F. F. Proctor.

The following year, Lent purchased the amphitheatre from Platt and instituted major renovations. The ring and front rows of seats were lowered and a hanging gallery was added, increasing the total capacity to 3,450. Permanent cages for the animals were installed beneath the seats and the façade was enlarged to hide the iron-work structure. The new façade held giant oil paintings of the activities in the ring and two busts of horse heads were mounted atop the main entrance.

In the years that followed, the best clowns and equestrians in the United States continued to appear at Lent's New York Circus. Austin was joined in the ring by such first-class comics as Joe Pentland and James Cooke, while Robert Stickney and Louise Tourniaire continued as featured equestrians. The major attractions of Lent's circus, however, were nationally known equestrians like The Great Melville,

Figure 30.   Interior of the Hippotheatron.
(Courtesy of the Billy Rose Theatre Collection, New York Public Library)

"The Daring Bare Back Steeplechase Rider"; Carlotta De Berg, "The BEST LADY RIDER The World Has Ever Produced"; and Levi J. North, "The Apollo on Horseback."[13] North, who had established his reputation in 1839 by executing the first full somersault on the back of a running horse, made his last appearance at the age of 52 at Lent's.

With the best equestrian troupe in the country, the finest stable of trained horses available, and the top stars of the equestrian circuit, Lent's New York Circus consistently drew capacity audiences. Lent was, nevertheless, constantly concerned with the respectability of his establishment and regularly advertised that it was "UNEXCEPTIONALLY CONDUCTED . . . The Most Acceptable Place of Amusement in New York. At Nights Filled with Fashion, [with] Matinees Crowded by Ladies and Children."[14] Occasionally, however, the building was rented for less respectable male-oriented activities. In September 1866, for example, the amphitheatre was sublet for a 12-day billiard tournament.

In April 1869, Lent ceased presenting the New York Circus and changed the name of the building back to the Hippotheatron. He continued as manager, booking other circuses and specialty acts for the amphitheatre until the summer of 1872, when it was sold to P. T. Barnum. Barnum moved his entire menagerie into the Hippotheatron on November 18, but his stay on 14th St. was destined to be short-lived. On December 24, the amphitheatre burned, destroying his valuable menagerie, Charles White's trained dogs, and the costumes for countless shows. The fire cost Barnum over $300,000. Instead of rebuilding the arena, he sold the plot of land and moved what remained of his operation further uptown.

In October 1867, while the Hippotheatron was still in its heyday, a portion of Dr. Cheever's Church of the Puritans at the southwest corner of Broadway and 15th St. was converted into an amusement spot called Bunyan Hall. Under the management of J. W. Bain, J. Q. Maynard and Philip Phillips, the hall was the site of "The Pilgrim," an exhibit of 50 "panoramic paintings" (as the *Art Journal* labeled them) depicting scenes from Bunyan's *Pilgrim's Progress.* Showings were held twice daily, at 2:00 and at 8:00, with admission of 50ᶜ for the matinee and $1.00 for the evening.[15]

Each of the 50 paintings exhibited at Bunyan Hall was 12 ft. high and 18 to 26 ft. wide and depicted a single scene from the novel. Beneath each, a sign listed its title: "The Christian and his Family," "The Seven Devils," "The Gates of Pearl," "The Celestial City," etc. The pictures were accompanied by "explanatory lectures" delivered by Mr. Maynard, and a four-part "bill" of music, featuring both solo and choral renditions of hymns under the direction of Mr. Phillips. The final sequence of paintings, "The Grand Transfiguration Finale," featured, in addition to the accompanying lectures and music, "special mechanical effects and special lighting."[16]

"The Pilgrim" continued to attract large crowds to Bunyan Hall until March 23, 1868, when the exhibit was transferred to the Brooklyn Athenaeum where it was equally successful. Bunyan Hall was closed permanently and the Church of the Puritans was demolished in 1869 to make room for Tiffany and Company.

Amusement was also readily available on the sidewalks outside the Palace Garden, the Hippotheatron, and Bunyan Hall. With elegant theatres, restaurants, hotels, and stores concentrated in a few blocks, the area attracted people dependent upon the money to be gleaned from crowds. The so-called "beggar belt" extended from 14th to 23rd streets between Broadway and 6th Ave. in the late 1860s. The same area was popular with vendors of every possible kind of merchandise and provided a convenient and lucrative "stage" for many of New York's street entertainers.

Among street entertainers, the musician was by far the most common. Often he was a lone instrumentalist who set up on a street corner to take advantage of the congestion. There were: the one-man band, "playing Panpipes and other instruments, emphasizing effects by a bass drum and cymbals strapped to his back, both hands and feet in vigorous action"; the street cornet player, "attired in frock coat . . . and high silk hat," who roamed back and forth on Ladies' Mile (between 14th and 23rd streets); and the street accordian player.[17]

Frequently, the musician employed an assistant to collect money or perform while he played. Invariably, the organ grinder traveled with a gaudily attired monkey chained to his barrel organ, and the street-piano player often was "accompanied by a female gaily attired in Italian costume who did an obbligato on the tambourine, which latter also served to collect the public's offerings."[18] The street-piano player was frequently joined by young neighborhood girls who danced spontaneously to his tunes.

The street concert was a somewhat more elaborate form of street music. Groups of Italians with fiddles and a harp performed on street corners and also on excursion boats; Negro quartets sang hymns and spirituals; and the streets were alive with the waltzes and schottisches of the four- and five-member German bands that played throughout the city.

In the mid-nineteenth century, the organ grinder's monkey was not the only animal to perform on the streets of New York. Trained bears also roamed the city, guided by their masters. The bear "was led through the streets, with a ring through his nose, and a muzzel; [the master] in his gay costume, would sing and the bear would perform on his hind legs, mostly making circles in imitation of dancing."[19]

Just as today's street entertainers become identified with a particular location, many street performers in the 1860s claimed a specific "pitch." The regulars around Union Square included a young one-armed soldier who played his barrel organ near the northwest corner of the park and an older organ grinder on the southeast side who, years before, had his "pitch" given to him by his fellow street performers. When Lester Wallack needed an organ grinder for his production of *Rosedale* in 1863, the older man was engaged "to pass across and about the stage . . . at 9 o'clock as a part of his regular trip through the square."[20] A decade later, when variety houses were opening in the area and the square was becoming the center of the city's theatrical activities, the same organ grinder became a well-known figure at the Rialto.

7

Popular Entertainments During the Rialto Period, 1871-1900

By 1871, the beginning of Union Square's Rialto period, pleasure gardens had virtually disappeared from the city and most circuses, when they were not on the road, sought vacant lots further uptown, leaving the square to the variety artists.[1] In the decade before Tony Pastor brought big-time vaudeville to 14th St., three smaller variety houses—Robinson Hall, the Columbia Opera House, and Butler and Shook's Union Square Theatre—had already come and gone.

The first, Robinson Hall, was located in a converted mansion at 18 E. 16th St. between Broadway and 5th Ave. The theatre was opened as Allemania Hall on October 15, 1868, with Professor Rhodes' geological exhibition, "Earth and Man," and for a short period was used for concerts and lectures. Within a year of its opening, however, the concerts and lectures had disappeared and the building had become a dance hall. In 1870, a Mr. Robinson leased the property and converted the space into a 500-seat vaudeville theatre.[2]

In 1872, Robinson retired from full-time producing. He sublet the hall to Paul Guignet, who changed the name of the theatre to the Bijou and presented his first production, *Le Meurtrier de Théodore* (a version of *Who Killed Cock Robin?*) on February 29, 1872. Under Guignet's management, all performances, ranging from comedy to opera bouffe to vaudeville, were in French, as were the playbills for the Bijou.

During the two years Guignet sublet the hall, he was frequently forced to suspend his operation and temporarily vacate the theatre to make room for entertainments that Robinson had booked. When this happened, the building was again advertised as Robinson Hall. In September 1873, Robinson rented the theatre to J. F. McDonough and H. A. Earnshaw, who presented J. W. Bullock's Royal Marionettes from London, "Replete with Gorgeous Scenery, Glittering Appointments, Costly Wardrobe, . . . Mechanical Transformations," and free from any "objectionable features."[3] The advertisement for the marionettes also quoted Charles Dickens, who claimed "there is no class of Drama which they are not capable of executing—from the extremely humorous to the most pathetic." In November of the same year, Robinson sponsored a series of readings by Owen Marlowe entitled "Gems," and the following January he presented the Pickaninnies from London who "entertained in their tiny way . . . with songs, dances, operettas, etc."[4]

In August 1874, M. B. Leavitt, an ambitious producer known as "the can-can manager of Mme Rentz's Female Minstrels," became the proprietor of Robinson Hall. Changing the name of the theatre to the Parisian Varieties, he entered into direct competition with Metropolitan Hall, 585 Broadway, which was also presenting the can-can. Robinson Hall was advertised as the "Temple of Sensational Art [which] shines over all every evening at 8," and the entertainment was described as "funny, frenchy, spicy and sparkling."[5] The staples of the bill were Mme Rentz's troupe of scantily clad beauties in the can-can and burlesques such as "Free-Love Contretemps," a travesty of the Oneida community presented on November 6, 1875. The remainder of the bill was filled by standard variety acts (songs, clog dances, minstrel sketches, magicians, acrobats, etc.). Leavitt was also fond of tableaux vivants featuring Mme Rentz's company or visiting "artists," such as Mme Blanche's Celebrated Tableaux Vivants Troupe. In keeping with the "French" nature of his establishment, Leavitt, early in his tenancy, installed a Grand Café in the cellar of the building.

By October of his first season as manager, Leavitt had adopted a two-part bill, with the variety acts on the first half of the program and a featured burlesque or extravaganza as the second part. One of these sketches, "The Female Bathers, or Fun at Long Beach," premiered on October 26 and promptly caused controversy. Advertised as "The New Local Sensational Sketch, written expressly for this theatre, and Brimful of Mirth, Laughter, Ludicrous Situations, and a Highly Sensational Termination," the sketch depicted a naive "rube" from New England on the beach with a bevy of bathing beauties, and was unanimously interpreted by clergy and moralists as a clear sign of the "degeneracy of the times."[6] "The Female Bathers," however, was not without its admirers. In his autobiography, *Fifty Years in Theatrical Management,* Leavitt says that one of these admirers, Denman Thompson, was so entranced by the Yankee in the piece that he pirated the character, changed the character's name to Joshua Whitcomb, and claimed him as his own creation.[7]

During the 1875-76 season, Leavitt alternated tenancy with W. H. Woodley who, when he occupied the hall, instituted a four-part bill which was considerably "cleaner" than Leavitt's. The first three parts of Woodley's shows featured aerialists, skipping-rope dances, serio-comic songs, balletic divertissements, clog dances, and quick-change artists. The fourth segment was an afterpiece such as "The Two Orphincs," a burlesque of the popular play recently presented at the Union Square Theatre. Leavitt, during this period, continued with Mme Rentz and the can-can, advertising his establishment as "The Great Fountain of Originality from which Imitators Draw Their Ideas."

In the fall of 1876, both Leavitt and Woodley ceased production at the theatre. Thereafter, the fortunes of Robinson Hall declined precipitously, and there were frequent changes in management and in the name of the hall. J. W. Swords operated the theatre as the Criterion in December, but closed the house after one production. It reopened in April 1877 as a burlesque house, named the Parisian Vaudeville, and in May became the Sixteenth Street Theatre under the management of A. H. Sheldon, who mounted a production of *Sarah's Young Man.* Hoping to nullify the theatre's reputation as home of the can-can and suggestive tableaux vivants, Sheldon advertised that his production contained "No vulgarity. No can-can. No Statue Business."[8] Sheldon's noble intentions notwithstanding, two months later Robinson Hall ended its life as a theatre and the property was sold to the trustees of the Apprentices' Library.

In September of 1875, Leavitt had advertised in the *Clipper,* "The best entertainment in New York. . . . We challenge comparison." Leavitt's challenge was answered the same month by Jake Berry, the new manager of the Columbia Opera House at 99 Greenwich Ave., several blocks to the south and west of Robinson Hall. The Columbia Opera House had opened in August 1874, presenting a two-part variety bill which featured the Columbia Minstrels in the first part and clog dancers, jugglers, Dutch songs, trapeze artists, magicians, and living statuary in the second half. Despite claims that "Our Bouquet of Novelty Never Fades" and weekly rotation of the bills, patronage during the first season was poor.

The situation changed dramatically in 1875 when Berry assumed control of the Columbia Opera House, erected the Columbia Café adjacent to it, and replaced the Columbia Minstrels with "The Latest Parisian Novelties." Advertisements for the Columbia Opera House now claimed that, "Without egotism we can safely say that OUR PERFORMANCES cannot be surpassed."[9] Berry endeavored to match Leavitt by ending his own programs with burlesques (P. T. Barnum was a favorite target of these burlesques) and risqué afterpieces with such suggestive titles as "The Naughty Marchioness," "Cleopatra's Amours," or "Fifty Nice Girls in Naughty Sketches."

The following season, Berry increased his pressure on his competitor, Leavitt, announcing in the *Clipper* that during the summer his establishment had been "refitted at an expense of $15,000 and is now acknowledged to be the handsomest theatre in the city." In addition to redecorating the theatre, a billiard parlor and a restaurant had been incorporated into the Columbia Café. The renovations were not the only improvements that Berry initiated; five new extravaganzas—"The Turkish Bathers," "Female Models," "French Dancers," "A Woman's Adventures in a Turkish Harem," and "The Female Bathers"—were added to the theatre's "unsavory" repertoire. In the next edition of the *Clipper,* Leavitt retaliated, announcing that a new sketch "The Midnight Bathers," would be unveiled at his theatre during the week.

The Yankee character in Berry's version of "The Female Bathers"—probably pirated from Leavitt's theatre—was played by an unknown actor from New Hampshire named Denman Thompson. Thompson, who had begun his stage career the year before at Boston's Howard Atheneum, then one of the most famous variety houses in New England, recently had moved to New York. Learning of Berry's policy of trying out new acts at the Columbia Opera House on Monday nights, he contacted Berry and his variety sketch, titled "Joshua Whitcomb," was placed on a Monday night bill early in September 1876.

> Thompson's impersonation of the New England farmer was received with such signals of appreciation that he realized that success was within his grasp, and it was not very long before he obtained the engagement at the Columbia that proved so important in his career.[10]

Success came so rapidly, in fact, that by September 18, Thompson's Yankee farmer, his name now shortened to Josh Whitcomb, was included in "The Female Bathers." The sketch was immediately popular and Thompson's character "was rich in a humor that was broad enough to delight his wholly masculine audience" which, at some point during the season, included James M. Hill (then a Chicago clothing merchant, but later the manager of the Union Square Theatre).[11] Hill was so impressed by the potential of Thompson's character that he waited for the actor at the stage door after the show and treated him to dinner at a nearby restaurant. While dining, Hill outlined the development of "Josh Whitcomb" into a full length drama, *The Old Homestead,* which was to become one of the longest running plays of the nineteenth century.

Encouraged by the financial success of "The Female Bathers" and his other sketches, Berry undertook further improvements of the building, which had been renamed the American Alhambra. On March 17, 1877, Berry announced in the *New York Clipper* that an $11,000 renovation had been completed; a new and more spacious front entrance had been constructed; and that his theatre was "the safest and most beautiful little place of amusement in the city." While beautification may have been a secondary objective, in actual fact most of the renovations had been dictated by the local authorities who, if they were unable to close the theatre through monthly raids, attempted to close it by declaring it unsafe. Eventually, the police harassment paid dividends; on October 27, 1877, the *Clipper* carried the following announcement:

> Notice to the profession—the [Columbia Opera House] is no longer a variety theatre, but is devoted to the production of . . . drama and opera bouffe. . . . Variety artists will please consider silence a polite negative. Wanted—a few good useful DRAMATIC . . . ARTISTS for the season.[12]

After what he must have considered an appropriate period of presenting unobjectionable entertainment, Berry attempted to return to the titillating and sensational fare which had previously brought him capacity audiences. On February 16, 1878, the *Clipper* contained a small, unobtrusive advertisement inviting variety artists to apply for employment at the Columbia Opera House. Evidently, the police also read the *Clipper* that day because nine days later they raided the theatre for the first time in four months. Frustrated by the futility of trying to fight or outwit the authorities, Berry surrendered his lease to the building shortly thereafter.

Following Berry's departure, both the management and the name of the theatre changed frequently. In March 1878, John B. French leased the house, calling it French's Vaudeville Theatre, and staged *Ten Nights in a Bar-room* and an extravaganza titled "Amazonian Marches," an example of the balletic extravaganzas which had become popular in New York's variety halls following *The Black Crook.* The following month, J. Ogden Stevens and Sam E. Ryan were the lessees, presenting a version of *Uncle Tom's Cabin* with Josie Crocker as Topsy and Stevens playing both George Harris and Simon Legree. Following this production, the house was closed for the summer, reopening in November as the Folly Theatre. The name proved appropriate, for after the failure of the initial production, *Little Bo Peep,* the Columbia Opera House was permanently closed as a theatre, the building razed and a livery stable erected in its place.

In 1880, freaks or "natural curiosities," heretofore confined to the museums located on the Bowery and the lower regions of Broadway, were first exhibited within the boundaries of the Rialto. Before the end of the decade, three separate museums near Union Square—Bunnell's, Huber's, and Meade's Midget Hall—had exhibited their oddities to countless thousands of spectators. Of these, Bunnell's and Huber's were true dime museums, with two or more floors devoted to showing the proprietor's collection of rare or unusual animals, an assortment of oversized, undersized or deformed humans, and grisly or bizarre items such as human heads in formaldehyde, and a "Theatorium" where variety entertainments were staged continuously from opening to closing time. The third museum, Meade's Midget Hall, was simply a space for exhibiting "little people."

Bunnell's Museum (fig. 31) at the northwest corner of Broadway and 9th St. (771 Broadway and 767-773 E. 9th St.) was opened in December 1880. Its proprietor, George B. Bunnell, a pioneer museum manager, had served his apprenticeship with P. T. Barnum and had opened his first museum at 103-105 Bowery in 1876, where his principal attraction was a "Dante's Inferno" composed of wax figures, mechanical contrivances and "pictorial views."[13] Three years later, Bunnell moved his operation to 198 Bowery near Bleeker Street, and in December of the following year, he sold the building to Frank Uffner and George Middleton in order to move to Broadway and 9th St.[14] By October 1882, Bunnell, recognized as "The Legitimate Successor of the Great Barnum," had added a second museum, The Annex, in Brooklyn.

Bunnell's museum at Broadway and 9th St., nicknamed "The Hub," had been created from an existing four-story structure. The exterior walls were adorned with giant paintings of current attractions, flags identifying both the museum and its proprietor flew from the roof, the location of the theatre was painted on a false balustrade above the top floor, and entrances had been created from both Broadway and 9th St. Inside, the four original, rectangular floors had been reduced to three L-shaped floors, each subdivided into two separate rooms. Both rooms on the top floor were devoted to curiosities; the second story housed curiosities in one room and Bunnell's menagerie in a second; and the ground floor contained the theatrum and the museum's main hall.

Figure 31. George Bunnell's Hub Museum.
(*Courtesy of the Harvard Theatre Collection*)

On December 4, 1880 an advertisement in the *Clipper* announced that G. B. Bunnell's Great Show, "filled with Novel, Strange, Curious, and Marvelous Creations all combined to form a Grand New Museum," would open its doors on December 8 in spectacular fashion. Bunnell's attractions for the grand opening included: Mlle Antoinette, "The Long Haired Marvel"; Captain Costentenus, "the tattooed Greek"; Hannah Battersby, giantess; a talking bird with a human brain; a group of Zulus; seven calves born at one birth; and lectures on National History by Professor Hewiett. The opening bill also included Annie Jones, bearded girl; Nelson the boy juggler; and Captain Beach and Ida La Selle, "monarchs of the water." Appraising the opening, Bunnell declared the following week that the "museum is an Established Fact. . . . A Success from the Start."[15]

As successful as the opening might have been, Bunnell was not content to rest on his laurels. During the week of December 20-25, he exhibited no less than four giants in the same room and by the second week of January 1881, he had lured several prime attractions, including Chang (the Mighty Chinese Giant), away from Middleton's Museum, one of his competitors. He further consolidated his advantage in February, presenting humorist Alf Burnett in the theatrum, while in one of the Curiosity Rooms the ever-popular midgets, Admiral Dot and Major Atom, were exhibited in striking contrast to Chang, China's Giant, and Goshen, the Arab Giant, shown in the same hall.

By the end of his first season, Bunnell was presenting six to ten shows daily to over 3,000 spectators, and The Hub was acknowledged as New York's leading dime museum. Rivals were unable to compete with Bunnell's policy of remaining open during the summer and could not match the popularity and diversity of his attractions. During the next two seasons, these included the Ford brothers, "slayers of Jesse James, and annihilators of bandits"; a girl with two heads, four arms, and one body; a cat congress; Chinese musicians; a monkey circus; psychic gypsies; a pigeon show; an exhibition of ghosts; a fat man's show billed as "The Highly-Amusing Convention of Corpulency"; and a "three-headed songstress" who, one critic theorized, "might have come within one of being able to sing the quartette from *Rigoletto,* if her three voices were of the right qualities."[16]

The bill for April 21, 1882, affords a less spectacular, but more typical, view of Bunnell's daily operation. On that date the Curiosity Halls were exhibiting Choung Chi Lang (The King of Giants); Mme Choung Chi Lang (the first Chinese Lady of Rank ever exhibited); Dudley Foster, weight five pounds; Ashley Benjamin, leopard boy; Sir Walter Stuart, limbless man; Ku Wee, Maori chieftain; Irene Woodward, tattooed lady; an albino girl; a tribe of Zulus; flying foxes; a Punch and Judy show; a shadow pantomime; seven giants, three of whom were nearly eight ft. tall; and Bunnell's aquarium and menagerie.

The stage performances at 12 noon, 4, and 8 p.m. on the same date featured the ventriloquist, Clever Carroll; Herr Singerhoff, billed as the successor to Ole Bull; the La Porte Sisters, queens of song; John Irish, the champion of the bell harmonican; the improvising songster, Frank Morton; and Charles Chestra, the

India rubber man. Shows at 2:30, 5:30, and 9:30 p.m. began with a piano overture by Herr Wiggins, the museum's musical director, followed by glees, songs,
and jubilee hymns by the Quaker City Quartet; a demonstration of the Great London Ethoscope; Japanese Tommy impersonating Adelina Patti; and Ion Ferreya
(the Man Flute). The program concluded with a "laughable afterpiece" entitled
Grim Goblins.

The Hub flourished until 1883, when Bunnell surrendered his lease to the
building and moved his freaks, menagerie, and aquarium to the former Lucy
Rushton's Theatre, 724-728 Broadway, several blocks south of the Rialto. While
not as successful in his new theatre as he had been at The Hub, Bunnell remained
in business for four more years, retiring to Connecticut in 1887. Bunnell's old
museum at Broadway and 9th St., like many abandoned theatres of the period,
was converted to business purposes.

In contrast to the three floors of oddities and continuous variety at Bunnell's
was Meade's Midget Hall (also called The Midget Hall), situated in a converted
mansion on the northwest corner of 5th Ave. and 14th St. The enterprise was opened
in November 1887 by James Meade, who exhibited "little people," both midgets
and unusual babies. From the outset, The Midget Hall, which lasted only one season,
was intended strictly as an exhibition hall and Meade made no attempt to provide
variety entertainment.

The four-story building which housed Meade's attractions had been erected
in 1835 by William M. Halstead, founder of the Halstead, Haines and Company
drygoods firm and in the mid-1860s had been converted into a concert room called
Brewster's Hall. Although ideally located on 5th Ave., with society's favorite
restaurant, Delmonico's, directly across the street, Brewster's Hall was unsuccessful
and closed shortly after its opening concert.

The Midget Hall was only slightly more successful. Throughout his first season,
Meade presented only one bill of attractions (fig. 32). His "headliners" were two
midgets: the famous General Mite, reputed to have been smaller than either Tom
Thumb or Commodore Nutt; and Minnie Obum, never exhibited in public prior
to her introduction by Meade, but destined to become a major attraction later in
her career. The remainder of Meade's attractions were babies—both "infantile
prodigies and freaks of nature"—exhibited under the catch-all billing of the Great
National Baby Show. Meade's collection of babies was as impressive as Bunnell's
assortment of giants. It included a baby who weighed only three quarters of a pound
at birth, a baby "that fell from the 4th story and escaped uninjured," one that
was born after its mother's death, Chinese babies, Japanese babies, fat babies, skinny
babies, twins, triplets, and a baby born with teeth. In the end, however, the limita-
tions of Meade's operation—the lack of variety entertainment and only one set of
attractions for the entire season—proved fatal. The Midget Hall closed after its
first year and the building became a carpet warehouse.

The year after the debut and demise of Meade's Midget Hall, one of the most
famous dime museums in New York history opened on E. 14th St. adjacent to

Figure 32. Broadside for Meade's Midget Hall.
(Courtesy of the Billy Rose Theatre Collection, New York Public Library)

Lüchow's and directly across from the Academy of Music. The museum was the creation of George H. Huber, proprietor of Huber's Prospect Garden, an oyster and chop house established at 106-108 E. 14th St. in 1882. The Prospect Garden catered to the after-show crowd, advertising that it remained open until 4:00 a.m. during the theatre and ball seasons, providing food, drink, and music. In 1885, Huber added vaudeville to his late-night entertainments.

In 1888, Huber acquired the three buildings on E. 13th St. which abutted his 14th St. property, knocked down the walls between the buildings, and created an L-shaped complex five stories high and occupying five city lots (fig. 33). When the reconstruction had been completed, eight rooms outfitted with 5,000 sq. ft. of glass-fronted cases (collectively termed the Curio Hall) were provided for oddities; the top floor had been divided into rooms where "freaks of good character" were allowed to board; 2,000 sq. yd. of carpet covered the halls; and the "entire building [was] heated with steam [and] illuminated with electricity."[17]

The Theatorium in Huber's new establishment, quite likely the former vaudeville hall in the Prospect Garden, was situated on the second floor of the building and was divided into two levels, an orchestra and a balcony (figs. 34, 35). The auditorium was equipped with a small stage at the 13th St. end of the hall and was amply provided with exits, not only at the rear but also at the side and in the center of the orchestra. The latter led directly to a set of steps on 14th St. As added attractions, the Manhattan Oyster House and Restaurant adjoined the orchestra and a craftsman called the California Wire King worked in the balcony, making gold pins and bracelets for patrons while they waited. The California Wire King had a counterpart in the Curio Hall, a Mr. M. Kloker, who would engrave a customer's name on glass for a moderate price.

The theatre was opened on August 13, 1888, as Worth's Palace Museum with Professor E. M. Worth billed as a sole proprietor, C. A. Wilson serving as manager, and Huber as a silent partner. Huber's decision to form a partnership with Worth had been a practical one. Huber was a former hotel manager (the Fourth Street Hotel) and restaurateur with neither the experience nor the necessary attractions required for a successful museum; Worth was an established museum manager and publicly claimed ownership of "The Finest Collection of National, Oriental and Historical Curiosities in Existence" numbering over one million inanimate oddities. Worth's curios formed the nucleus of the museum's attractions and were mentioned repeatedly in the advertising during the first two years. One such advertisement declared:

> Professor Worth's collection . . . has a world-wide reputation for completeness and rarity. . . . His collection furnishes just what the moral and religious portion of the community want—an unobjectionable place of amusement, where everyone can go and be highly entertained, instructed and satisfied.[18]

Figure 33. Huber's Museum.
*(Courtesy of the Theatre Collection,
Museum of the City of New York)*

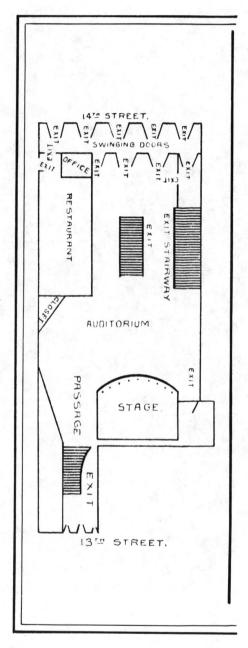

Figure 34.   Orchestra of the Theatorium at Huber's Museum.
(Courtesy of the Harvard Theatre Collection)

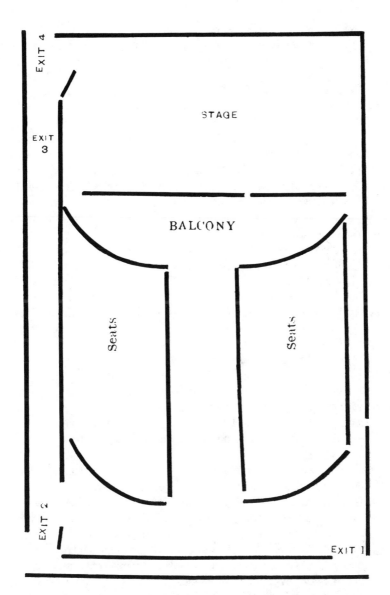

EXIT 4

EXIT 3

STAGE

BALCONY

Seats

Seats

EXIT 2

EXIT 1

Exits Nos. 1 and 2 lead to 13th Street.
Exits Nos. 3 and 4 lead to 14th Street.

Figure 35.   Balcony of the Theatorium at Huber's Museum.
(Courtesy of the Harvard Theatre Collection)

Worth and Huber, however, were not content to offer only one type of attraction, regardless of how extensive or unusual. At the time the museum opened, the trade newspapers carried the following appeal,

> We want at all times, Recognized Artists for the Theatorium, Living Curiosities, Trained Animals and Mechanical Novelties of Merit, as we desire to present our patrons as many new features as may be offered. Write or telegraph for dates.[19]

Meanwhile, advertisements for the museum in the daily newspapers announced "hourly performances . . . especially adapted for Ladies and Children—10ᶜ Admission," and the stage during the first months of operation was occupied continuously by a succession of whistlers, ventriloquists, magicians, sand and clog dancers, mind readers, sword swallowers, fire eaters, vocalists, and wrestling matches between men and bears.

While variety artists of all sorts flocked to Worth's for employment, freaks were more difficult to engage and for the first months of operation the museum's Curio Hall was empty. Early advertisements contain no mention of natural oddities and Odell's chronicle lists October 29—when Jo Jo (the Dog-Faced Boy), Kit Kit (the Fiji Princess and Queen of the Midgets), and Big Eliza (the Fat Negress) were displayed—as the first date for an exhibit in the Curio Hall. From that date, however, Worth and Huber's list of natural wonders expanded rapidly. Within months George Williams (the Turtle-boy), Ivan D. Osloff (the Transparent Man), John R. Bass (the Ossified Man), Col. Pickett Nelson (the Largest Living Man), J. W. Coffey (the Skeleton Dude), Charles Elsworth (Blind Checker Player), William McKenna (the Human Ostrich), and Andy Gaffney (Skeleton Giant) had filled vacant spaces in the Curio Hall, as had an assortment of cannibals, midgets, Zulus, horses of different sizes, giants, tattooed people, and a tribe of Indians in encampment.

Two of Worth and Huber's freaks, Barney Baldwin (the Anatomical Paradox) and Coffey (the Skeleton Dude), proved to be the first season's most popular attractions. Baldwin, a former railroad switchman who had broken his neck in an accident and had survived, wore a special brace to hold his head erect when not on stage. On exhibit without his brace, his head dropped nearly to his stomach. Coffey, who had advertised in local newspapers for a "plump and pleasing" wife, left the museum in May to be married in violation of his contract. When Worth threatened to sue, Coffey returned to the museum with his bride, and the Skeleton Dude and his plump wife drew large crowds until the close of the season in June.

By January 1890, Huber had graduated from silent to full partnership and the theatre had been renamed Worth and Huber's Palace Museum. The arrangement, however, was short-lived, for the *Clipper* on April 12 carried the announcement that they had dissolved their partnership. Huber became sole proprietor of the theatre, while Worth moved uptown to 6th Ave. and 13th St. where he established E. M. Worth's Model Museum and Family Theatre. Ironically, the same month that the partnership was dissolved, Huber opened a new 1,000-seat theatorium, the Auditorium Annex, which had taken almost six months to complete.[20]

Under Huber's management, the museum (called Huber's Palace Museum from 1890 to 1901 and Huber's Museum from 1901 to 1910) flourished and for two decades his freaks and variety entertainers were the best available. During this period, such well-known variety peformers as Weber and Fields, May and Flo Irwin, the Rogers Brothers, James T. Powers (who had begun his stage career at the Columbia Opera House and later achieved a distinguished reputation in the legitimate theatre), and Princess Rajah (later a headliner at Hammerstein's Victoria) brought their acts to the Annex stage. So impressive was Huber's reputation that when Princess Rajah opened uptown in 1904, Hammerstein billed her as "Direct from Huber's to Hammerstein's."

Huber was equally proud of the freaks he exhibited during the museum's golden years and he continually upgraded his "collection" by maintaining a battery of scouts who, whenever rumors of a new oddity were heard, immediately investigated the claims. "'All of my freaks are genuine,' Mr. Huber was wont to say, [adding] as an afterthought, 'almost all of them.'" [21] By 1895, the Oregon Wonder (a horse with an enormous mane), Moth Miller (a horse with a golden tooth), Myrtle Corbett (the Four-Legged Woman), a set of twins with two heads and one body, and a midget billed as the second Tom Thumb had been added to the list of attractions in the Curio Hall, which still included the Ossified Man, the Turtle Boy and many others who had joined the museum's company in its first year.

In June 1910, the museum closed for the summer months, as was the custom. The following month, Huber announced that he had released the freaks and variety performers from their contracts and that the museum would not reopen. Although publicly citing his desire to devote more time to his theatre at 162nd St. and Jerome Ave. as the reason for abandoning 14th St., most likely Huber, like Tony Pastor two years before, was finding it increasingly difficult to compete with the growing number of movie houses nearby. Shortly after the announcement, the property was purchased by Albert Lüchow, who converted the ground floor of the museum into additional space for his restaurant.

The panorama, which had been declining in popularity during the 1860s and 1870s, briefly reappeared in the Union Square area in 1887. In that year, a panorama called the Cyclorama of Gettysburg opened to the public in a specially constructed, circular, iron building on 4th Ave. between 18th and 19th streets (fig. 36). The building located on the former Matthews estate, cost $29,000 to erect, with an additional $12,000 spent for electrical installation.[22] The painting itself (fig. 37) was created by the well-known French artist Paul Philippoteaux at the cost of $75,000. Prior to its presentation by the Union Square Panorama Company, it had been exhibited in Brooklyn for two years, yielding an annual profit estimated in excess of $40,000.

Once inside the panorama hall, "the spectator stood on what was supposed to be a central position in the field—on a platform built over an embankment of

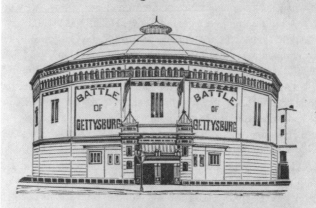

THE GREATEST WORK OF THE CELEBRATED FRENCH ARTIST,

PAUL PHILIPPOTEAUX.

Battle of ✸ ✸ ✸ ✸

Gettysburg,

UNION · SQUARE, · NEW · YORK,

(Fourth Avenue, 18th and 19th Streets.)

Open from 9 A. M. to 11 P. M.   Sundays Included.

— ADMISSION. —

ADULTS, 50 CTS.   CHILDREN, 25 CTS.

PRESS OF BROOKLYN DAILY EAGLE.

Figure 36.   Union Square Panorama Building. This building housed
the Gettysburg cyclorama.
(Courtesy of The New York Historical Society, New York City)

Figure 37.   Section of the Gettysburg Panorama.
(Harper's Weekly)

real earth, while all around on an immense canvas was unfolded the clash of the contending forces."[23] The space between the platform and the canvas was strewn with actual relics of the war (cannon, wagons, rifles, saddles, etc.), and a tour of the battlefield was guided by a survivor of Gettysburg in uniform. The gigantic painting itself, supposedly the best ever rendered by Philippoteaux, was "a masterpiece of realism . . . true to nature and history in all respects. . . . The line between painting and 'props' [was] indistinguishable."[24] The sense of reality was heightened by an elaborate and carefully orchestrated set of special effects—explosions, flashes of lights, gunshots, puffs of smoke, and screams of agony.

The panorama opened in December 1887 and quickly became popular, not only with the usual New York amusement seekers and tourists eager to sample the city's entertainment, but with Civil War veterans who would visit with their relatives and describe the battle as they remembered it. In March 1888, the *Amusement Gazette* announced "the Battle of Gettysburg is now drawing crowds of people who follow a fashion in amusements. It has been decided that a panorama is an orthodox Lenten amusement. Therefore, panorama-going is the fashion."[25]

The Cyclorama of Gettysburg continued to attract large crowds until 1892 when it was removed, sent to Washington, and installed in the Bull Run Building. During its four years on Union Square, more than one million spectators viewed the battle of Gettysburg and the Union Square Panorama Company realized an average annual profit of $85,000.[26] Shortly after the original canvas was removed, the company installed a panorama of Niagara Falls. The new panorama, however, failed during its first year and the Union Square Panorama Company ceased operation. The site of the panorama hall is now occupied by an office building. The failure of the Niagara Falls panorama, however, did not mark the end of optical shows on Union Square; fewer than 10 years later, another optical device, the motion picture, was exhibited at Keith's Union Square Theatre, heralding a new era of popular entertainment on 14th St.

8

The Theatrical Support Businesses

The nucleus of the Rialto had been formed in the 1860s with the opening of Wallack's, the Fourteenth Street Theatre, Tammany Hall, Irving Hall, and Steinway Hall. The square, however, did not become the center of theatrical activity until the 1870s, when businesses created specifically to provide goods and services for the theatre became concentrated in the area. Many of these enterprises (costume houses, agents' offices, publishing houses, theatrical newspapers, photographers, and printers) had been established in earlier decades, and during the 1860s were spread along Broadway from City Hall to 8th St. and along the entire length of the Bowery.

Beginning in the late 1860s and early 1870s, support businesses began to invade the Union Square area, moving into nearby brownstones and empty shops. In 1878 the *New York World* noted their concentration in the neighborhood, stating that "there is no doubt that for the present at least Union Square has been captured by people and things dramatic."[1] The proliferation of theatre-related enterprises prompted the *World* to proclaim the square the city's dramatic center.

The Rialto's first theatre-related enterprise, the Eaves Costume Company, was housed in a three-story building at 63 E. 12th St. The firm was founded in 1867 by Albert G. Eaves, a former actor, whose experience on the stage gave him a thorough first-hand knowledge of costuming, and whose stage colleagues furnished his initial clientele. One of the first to have his costumes made by Eaves was Edwin Booth, who purchased an entire wardrobe for *Hamlet* shortly after the establishment opened.

In the remaining years of the century, Eaves' company, nicknamed "The Old Stand," developed into one of the leading costume houses in the country, with a clientele that included such stalwarts of the late nineteenth-century stage as John Drew, Stuart Robson, Joseph Jefferson, Richard Mansfield, Otis Skinner, Mrs. Fiske, and Ada Rehan. According to his advertisements, Eaves furnished "every requisite for theatres . . . wigs, beards, shoes, boots, tights, swords, etc.," and defied competition in "price, style or workmanship."[2] Upon his death in 1900, his son Colin S. Eaves, became president of the firm, moved the company to larger quarters at 151 W. 46th St. and continued to increase its reputation.

Following Colin Eaves' death in 1909, the firm was purchased by Charles Geoly, who expanded its operation by outfitting not only the stars of the legitimate stage but entire casts of such extravaganzas as the "Ziegfeld Follies," Earl Carroll's "Vanities," and D. W. Griffith's films. In the succeeding decades, the Eaves Costume Company added Paramount Pictures to its growing list of customers and claimed such notable credits as Valentino's costumes in *Monsieur Beaucaire* and *Sainted Devil*, Orson Welles' tunic in *Romeo and Juliet*, Helen Hayes' gowns for *Victoria Regina*, and Vivien Leigh's $1,200 embroidered chiffon and satin gown in *Tovarich*.[3] In 1981, Eaves merged with the Brooks-Van Horn Company. Today, the Eaves-Brooks Costume Company, Inc., managed by Daniel Geoly and located at 423 W. 55th St., is a multi-million dollar corporation with an inventory of over 100,000 costumes stored in a huge warehouse in Long Island City, Queens.

During the 1870s, Eaves lost his monopoly of the Union Square area. In 1871 a small firm, Jacoby and Company, Costumers, was opened at 868 Broadway between 17th and 18th streets; by the end of the decade, three more costume houses occupied quarters in the neighborhood. Koehler's Costume Shop, originally established at 346 Bowery by Francis Koehler, moved into a converted brownstone at 2 Union Square (fig. 38) in 1875 and continued operation well into the twentieth century under the management of Amelia Koehler, the founder's wife. In 1878 Ben Rose Costumes leased space several doors north of Jacoby and Company at 872 Broadway and Koehler acquired a new neighbor at 8 Union Square: A. Roemer and Son, Theatrical Costumes (later F. Roemer, Costumer). The latter firm, which moved from 55 E. 4th St., claimed to be the "Largest Historical Costumer and Armorer in America," and was costumer for the Fifth Avenue Theatre, the Grand Opera House, the Star Theatre, Madison Square Garden, Niblo's Garden, the New Park Theatre, People's Theatre, and the Fourteenth Street Theatre.[4]

The influx of costume houses into the area continued during the succeeding decade, with five additional companies joining the existing five. Three of these newcomers specialized in specific items of dress: Charles Meyer, Wigmaker, at 123 4th Ave. near 12th St.; Charles Winkelmann, Wigmaker, at 10 Union Square; and Nestrock Theatrical Shoes, 12 Union Square. The remaining two, Bloom's Theatrical Supplies Emporium and Dazian's Theatrical Emporium, were among the city's largest and most successful costume houses.

Bloom's, "The Great American Theatrical Headquarters," for many years located at 338-340 Bowery, announced its removal to 48-50 W. 14th St. in the *Clipper* of December 4, 1880. Evidently Bloom was fearful of losing old customers, for early in 1881 his advertisements carried the assurance that the company still carried anatomical symmetricals, hose, tights, body shirts, leotards, shoes, hats, wigs, theatrical jewelry, swords, shields, and daggers, and still maintained its collection of over 5,000 costume plates.[5] Later in the same year, Isaac Bloom announced that he was leaving the parent firm and would open his own store, the Fifth Avenue Emporium, at 124 5th Ave. between 17th and 18th streets. According to his advertisements, the new company offered many of the same goods and services as the original store.

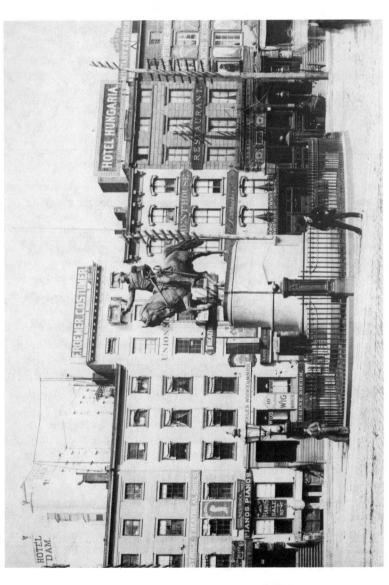

Figure 38. Numbers 2-12 Union Square. Shows Nestrock, Theatrical Shoes; Charles Winkelman, Wigmaker; and the Roemer and Koehler Costume Companies; also visible are the Hotel Hungaria and the Monument House (partially hidden by the statue of Washington). The *Dramatic Mirror* had offices in number 12 Union Square, at the extreme left of the picture. (*Courtesy of The New York Historical Society, New York City*)

When Dazian's Theatrical Emporium moved to a five-story building at 26 Union Square (fig. 39) in 1882, it was already one of the oldest and largest theatrical suppliers in the city. The firm was established in 1842 as a "Fancy and Dry Goods" store at 4½ Marion St. (now Lafayette St.) by Wolf Dazian, a young Bavarian immigrant. Shortly after opening his business, Dazian decided to specialize in the "glitter and glamour fabrics" popular on the stage. The following year, P. T. Barnum contracted Dazian to build a wardrobe for "Mlle Fanny," a giant orangutan, with instructions that no expense be spared in making his star the best-dressed female in America. Photographs of the ape dressed in an elegant gown, wearing a hat topped with ostrich feathers and carrying a parasol, were released to the public, and Dazian's reputation was established. Barnum returned in 1850 to order a Dazian gown for Jenny Lind, and when William Wheatley needed to costume the cast of *The Black Crook* in 1866, he hired Dazian, the only costumer in New York who carried the materials for ballet costumes.

When the theatres moved uptown, Dazian followed, first to the Bowery in 1871, and then to Union Square in 1882. The salon on the first floor of his Union Square headquarters soon became a popular gathering place for actors in the neighborhood. One reporter, during periodic trips to Dazian's, documented visits by Sarah Bernhardt, Salvini, Coquelin, Modjeska, Mrs. Leslie Carter, Augustin Daly, and Charles Dillingham, as well as a recital by Josef Hoffman. A second journalist noted that Dazian's windows, "bursting with armor and ass's heads (for *A Midsummer Night's Dream*) and bedizened with open-work lace," acted like a magnet, attracting actors strolling through the square.[6]

Many of the actors attracted to his salon by the magnificence of his shop windows or the possibility of a social encounter eventually became customers. While his shop was located on Union Square, Dazian numbered among the stars he costumed Edwin Booth, Adelina Patti, Lillian Russell, Henry Irving, Joseph Jefferson, Sarah Bernhardt, and Richard Mansfield. During this period he also expanded his operation to include the building of wardrobes for Grand Opera, Spectacle, Opera Bouffe, Comic Opera, Circus, Mardi Gras, Tableaux, and Processions. Dazian costumes were used exclusively by the Metropolitan Opera Company; Barnum and Bailey elephants sported Dazian-designed ballet skirts; and his symmetricals were standard equipment for performers from "The Divine Sarah" to the most obscure chorine.

In 1902 Dazian moved to W. 44th St., and on his death, his son, Henry, became president of the firm. Under his leadership, the company ceased making costumes in 1919, choosing to supply materials to other costume shops. Dazian's also became a frequent and important backer of Broadway shows. Currently, Dazian, Inc., maintains offices in Boston, Chicago, St. Louis, and Hollywood, in addition to headquarters in New York and Dallas.

The evolution of theatre into big business in the mid-nineteenth century coincided with developments in the science of photography, and the nineteenth-century theatrical photographer became a prominent member of the entertainment support

Figure 39. Dazian's Theatrical Emporium. 26 Union Square.
*(Courtesy of the Billy Rose Theatre Collection,
New York Public Library)*

industry. People enjoyed collecting photos of the stars of the stage and entertainers quickly realized that publicity photographs could advance their careers. These publicity pictures first took the form of the *carte de visite*, a studio photo printed on a 2½ by 4 in. card; later they appeared as 4½ by 6 in. "cabinet photos."

The subsequent boom in theatre photography in the 1870s and 1880s made the names of Napoleon Sarony, Benjamin Falk, George C. Rockwood, and José Mora household words, and hundreds of other New York photographers advertised "Theatrical Portraits a Specialty." Photographers of the era actively solicited "sittings," often paying celebrities for the exclusive right to display and to distribute their portraits publicly, and it was not uncommon for a star to receive over $1,000 for a single session.

When Union Square became the center of dramatic activities, a number of theatrical photographers opened studios in the neighborhood in order to be close to their clientele and to exhibit their work to the acting profession and the theatre-going public. At various times during the three decades that the square was the city's Rialto, a number of photographers maintained studios near the square, including Napoleon Sarony (37 Union Square), Carl Hecker (46 E. 14th St.), Charles Eisenmann (18th W. 14th St.), the Bogardus Gallery (16 W. 14th St.), Feinberg Photo Studio (16 W. 14th St.), Andrew Jordan (867-869 Broadway), Pach Brothers' Gallery (841 Broadway), and Benjamin Falk (347 E. 14th St.).[7] Some, like Pach Brothers, included theatrical photographs in their general portrait work; others, like Sarony and Falk, specialized in the stage and stage personalities. Falk, in addition to taking studio portraits, is credited with being the first to photograph a complete scene on stage.

Occasionally, photographers specialized in a particular aspect of theatrical photography. In the late 1870s, Feinberg, Bogardus, and Eisenmann, for example, produced a large proportion of the *cartes de visite* for dime museums. P. T. Barnum was among the first to sit for Eisenmann at his 14th St. studio. In the 1880s Eisenmann, who advertised himself as "The Popular Photographer," became the semi-official photographer of midgets and other freaks. His clients included Major Mite, Dudley Foster, the Adams Sisters, and Chiquita.

The most famous theatrical photographer of the era, however, was Napoleon Sarony. Before the Civil War, he had already established a reputation as an accomplished lithographer and was learning photography from his brother, Oliver, a prominent London photographer. In 1866, he abandoned lithography to concentrate upon photographing stars of the stage, and opened his first studio at 630 Broadway. Five years later, when he moved to 37 Union Square (fig. 40), he was in the first echelon of theatrical photographers.

In the 24 years Sarony was in his Union Square studio, he became the undisputed leader among theatrical photographers and was regarded by his colleagues as "the father of artistic photography in America." Sarony took photography from the realm of science and "placed it upon the pedestal of art" by introducing painted backgrounds and unusual props into his pictures, by posing his subjects in a variety

Figure 40. 37 Union Square. This building housed Napoleon Sarony's studio. Note Brentano's Literary Emporium at 33 Union Square, to the left of Sarony's studio.
(Courtesy of the Print Archives, Museum of the City of New York)

of new and more dramatic poses, and by working for hours to capture "what was characteristic and picturesque in his subjects . . . and [to make] these features predominant in his pictures."[8] As a businessman, he was without equal. He would pursue a potential subject relentlessly and would make "deals" which his competitors were unable to match. In 1882, for example, Sarony paid $5,000 for the exclusive right to photograph Lillie Langtry.

In his personal life, Sarony became almost as famous and as colorful as the stars he photographed. Well known as an eccentric, the 5 ft. 1 in.-tall Sarony, bearded and mustached, often paraded Broadway dressed in a black overcoat with a broad collar and large sealskin cuffs, or riding breeches, cavalry boots, a calfskin jacket, and a Turkish fez. A bohemian outside the studio, he was an energetic martinet when at work. In his studio, "he functioned as producer, director and stage manager, positioning the camera, posing the subject, arranging light screens, draperies and accessories, and barking orders to his assistants, while actors and actresses responded to his enthusiastic direction with brief but intense performances before the camera."[9]

Sarony's studio was as unique as its proprietor. The front windows, crammed with recent photographs of stage celebrities, attracted crowds eager to see the latest pictures and possibly spy one of Sarony's famous clients. His customers reached his studio on the top floor of the building via a slow elevator and when they disembarked, entered a reception room described as "a sort of dumping ground of the dealers in unsaleable idols, tattered tapestry, and indigent crocodiles."[10] Every inch was cluttered with paintings and bric-a-brac. Scattered at random throughout the room were Russian sleighs, Indian pottery, Japanese armor, Egyptian mummies, and medieval weapons and statues.

In contrast to the flamboyance of the reception room, Sarony's studio, like most photographers' studios of the period, was simply a large loft which housed his equipment. The room was topped by an enormous skylight fitted with blinds to control the sunlight, the principal source of light for the nineteenth-century photographer. According to one customer, the loft "was filled with glare, bareness, screens, iron instruments of torture," and the odors of various chemicals.[11]

In 1895, the year before he died, Sarony abandoned his studio on Union Square and moved to 256 5th Ave. After his death, his son, Otto, who had been his father's business manager for years, continued the business at the 5th Ave. address. The building at 37 Union Square, with a new façade added, is still standing.

If Americans in the late nineteenth century avidly collected photos of their favorite stars, they were equally eager to read about them and to keep abreast of important events in the world of the stage. To satisfy this curiosity, theatrical newspapers and magazines, many published in the Union Square area, were distributed nationwide. Some, like *Leslie's Sporting and Dramatic Times,* divided their space between athletics and the drama; others, like the *Dramatic Mirror,* were devoted solely to the theatre.

Beginning in the mid-1870s, theatrical publications began moving into the vicinity of Union Square and by the early eighties, the following journals were in operation: *The Stage,* located at 46 E. 14th St.; the *Musical Courier,* situated at 25 E. 14th St.; *The Dramatic News,* 866 Broadway, and *The Dramatic Times,* 860 Broadway, both published by C. A. Byrn; the *Illustrated Dramatic Weekly,* edited by Sidney Rosenfeld, at 120 Union Square. *The Dramatic Magazine* maintained offices at 816 Broadway; *Leslie's Sporting and Dramatic Times* occupied quarters at 35 E. 17th St.; *Music: A Review of Stage, Art, Literature and Society* (*Freund's Music and Drama* after 1883) was published at 30 E. 14th St.; and, the *Dramatic Mirror* occupied the top floor of a building at 12 Union Square.

For 40 years the *Mirror* was one of America's pre-eminent theatrical newspapers and its pages document "the history of the American stage . . . during the final decades of the [nineteenth] century."[12] Its first issue, an unpretentious eight-page edition with a crude engraving of Tony Pastor on page one, was printed on January 4, 1879. The remainder of the first issue, then called the *New York Mirror,* was devoted to advertisements and a list of attractions at city theatres. In February 1880, the size of the paper was increased to 12 pages to accommodate the growing number of advertisements, and in July of the same year, Harrison Grey Fiske was first listed as editor, although he had been serving in that capacity for some time.

Shortly thereafter, the *Mirror,* which was published every Tuesday and was becoming a leading theatrical newspaper, added reviews by A. C. Wheeler ("Nym Crinkle"), biographies, obituaries, and a correspondence page. In the mid-1880s, Fiske, through his editorials, began to campaign for reforms in the theatre. In 1885, the *Mirror* supported the newly founded Actors' Fund; in 1887, it crusaded against play-pirates; and when the Theatrical Syndicate was formed in the late 1890s, the *Mirror* was in the vanguard of its opposition.[13] In 1887, the *Mirror* moved from Union Square to 145 5th Ave. and four years later moved again, to Broadway and 40th St. Fiske continued to edit the paper until his retirement in 1911 and the paper, under corporate management after Fiske left, remained prominent until 1921 when it ceased publication.

Beginning in the mid-nineteenth century, the selling of play scripts became a lucrative venture and quickly attracted enterprising businessmen, who opened shops throughout the city. The protection afforded by the 1856 Copyright Law, which granted playrights the "sole right . . . to act, perform or represent their works," encouraged many writers to release their plays for publication and sale to an eager public. Scripts were purchased not only by professional actors and managers seeking a new attraction, but by amateur dramatic groups and the reading public alike. In an age when public libraries were few, these shops quickly became the Meccas of the city's readers—both the elite and the "commonplace and earthy folk."

By the time the *World* declared Union Square the hub of theatrical activities, the neighborhood already had three script sellers: Christern's, Brentano's Literary Emporium, and Samuel French & Son. Christern's, located just off the square at 77 University Place, specialized in imported scripts. The store, opened in 1876 by Frederick Christern, quickly became well known for its extensive stock of French plays and was a principal supplier of scripts for the French theatre in New York. Christern's stay on the square, however, was relatively short. In 1880, he closed the shop on University Place, moving uptown to 23rd St.

Brentano's Literary Emporium opened at 33 Union Square (fig. 41) in 1876, soon becoming New York's most famous and popular literary store where fashionable book buyers routinely gathered. Like Sarony's studio and Dazian's salon, Brentano's was a popular rendezvous for the theatre's elite, who met to exchange the latest news, "while the more serious browsed at leisure and finally bought a volume or two."[14]

The rise of the store's founder, Agosto Brentano, was one of the better-known Horatio Alger stories of the period. An immigrant from Sicily, Brentano persuaded the proprietor of the New York Hotel to let him open a small newspaper stand, provided by the *New York Sun,* on the sidewalk out front. In 1860, Brentano invested his meagre earnings to import copies of the *London Times* which carried an account of the John C. Heenan-Tom Sayers fight in England. After personally receiving the newspapers at the dock, Brentano sold the first available accounts of the world championship bout, fought 42 rounds to a draw, for $1.00 each.[15] With the profits from this venture, Brentano opened a larger stand in Union Square, moving to a small store at 5 Union Square in 1870. There he sold foreign and domestic newspapers, the leading periodicals, and tickets for transatlantic voyages.

Having prospered in his first shop, Brentano took his brothers and son into the business and in 1876 moved further up the square to number 33. In his new emporium, Brentano added books and playscripts to his inventory, while continuing to carry foreign newspapers and a complete stock of periodicals. By the time he moved further uptown in 1893, the foundation of a chain of bookstores bearing his name had been laid. Shortly after his departure, Brentano's famous emporium at 33 Union Square was demolished and the Union Building was erected in its place.

Two blocks to the south, Samuel French and Son, already a leading publisher of playscripts, maintained its New York office. The firm's founder, Samuel French, had begun simply, selling Mammoth Weeklies (comparable to today's paperbacks) on New York streets during the 1837 Depression. In 1846, after an apprenticeship with William Taylor and Company, publishers of American and British plays, French established his own company at 293 Broadway, accepting routine printing jobs to finance his small business. At the same time, French was purchasing every available set of printing plates for plays, including those owned by his former employer. In 1850, French moved to 151 Nassau Street and four years later, with the publication of his first catalogue, *French's American Drama,* he announced his specialization in play publishing.

By the end of the decade, French had acquired a substantial proportion of the existing printing plates, thus absorbing his competitors and virtually monopolizing the play-publishing industry in New York. The company's inventory was over 100,000 plays, which were listed in two catalogues, *French's Standard Drama* and *French's Minor Drama,* and included first editions of the George L. Aiken version of *Uncle Tom's Cabin* and *The Poor of New York* by Dion Boucicault.[16]

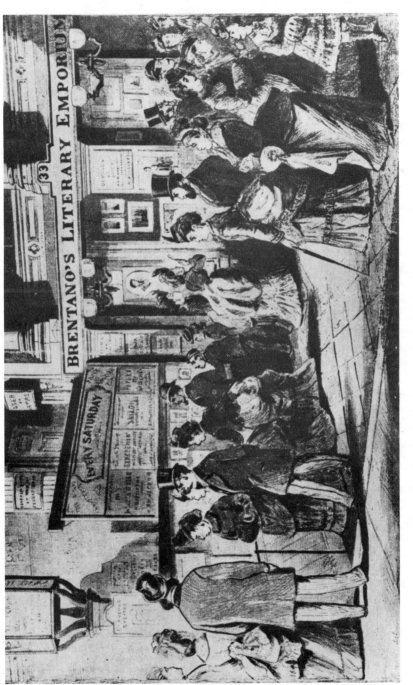

Figure 41. Brentano's Literary Emporium. 33 Union Square.
(*Courtesy of the Print Archives, Museum of the City of New York*)

French's early success also stemmed from his support of amateur theatre: "from his premises on Nassau Street . . . he supplied everything the budding amateur dramatic group might need . . . apart from acting ability, and he even tried to supply that in the form of how-to-act books."[17] According to a company advertisement, the list of items available to amateur groups included temperance plays, drawing room plays, Ethiopian plays, guide books, speakers' pantomimes, tableaux lights, magnesium lights, colored fire, burnt cork, theatrical face preparations, wigs, beards, moustaches, costumes, scenery, and charades.

In 1870, French brought his only son, Thomas Henry French, into the business; when the elder French moved to England two years later to assume control of Thomas Lacy's London play publishing firm, Thomas became sole manager of the New York office. The opening of a London office gave the firm, now named Samuel French and Son, a significant advantage over other companies as "Samuel in England was able to acquire the American rights of many English and continental plays, and Thomas Henry, as an American citizen, was able to exploit them."[18] The company's international status spurred the Frenches to lobby for an international copyright law and was instrumental in the eventual adoption of the Chase Act in 1891, which guaranteed protection to foreign authors.

The New York office of the firm remained on Nassau Street until 1878 when it moved to 38 E. 14th St. just east of University Place, which afforded the Frenches more warehouse space and provided a larger, more attractive script store (fig. 42). In addition to the French catalogue of plays, the inventory in the new quarters included the Davidson, Cumberland, Webster, Lacy, and Spencer series of plays imported from England.

In the same year that the Union Square office was opened, Thomas French entered the ranks of New York theatre managers, leasing the New Park Theatre for one season. During the following decade, he held short-term leases for the Grand Opera House on 23rd St., in partnership with Frank L. Sanger, and the Broadway Theatre, in addition to financing a national tour of the Lillian Russell Opera Company and four road companies of *Little Lord Fauntleroy*. When Madison Square Garden opened in 1890, Thomas French was listed as a co-manager with his father, and three years later he built the American Theatre on 42nd St. which specialized in extravaganzas. French lost the American in 1897 as the result of a foreclosure judgment.

The company remained on Union Square until 1887 when it moved to W. 23rd Street, first to number 19 and then to 24-26 in 1896. The firm subsequently moved to 28 W. 38th St. in 1910 and finally to its present quarters at 25 W. 45th St. in 1924. Currently named Samuel French, Inc. (Samuel French Ltd. in England and Canada) and under the direction of Abbott Van Nostrand, chairman of the board, the firm maintains offices in New York, Hollywood, Toronto, London, and Brookvale, England.

The printing and distribution of sheet music also gained prominence in the second half of the nineteenth century. Before the mass production of the phonograph,

Figure 42. Play Store of Samuel French and Son. 38 E. 14th St.
(Author's Collection)

parlors throughout America contained a piano around which families gathered for an evening's enjoyment, and purveyors of musical scores furnished sheet music to the country.

The center of the country's music publishing industry, later dubbed Tin Pan Alley, had its beginnings on Union Square during the 1870s. Novello, Ever and Company at 21 E. 17th St. sold a full line of English, German, and French scores and orchestral parts; Boosey and Company, 3 E. 14th St., supplied "scores of every known opera"; Edward Schuberth and Company's Foreign and American Music Depot, situated at 27 Union Square, carried "all works of merit of classical and modern composers"; and Gustave Schirmer, Importer and Publisher of Music, maintained a shop at 35 Union Square between Brentano's and Sarony's studio.[19] Nearby, Edward Hopkins ran a small publishing firm at 30 E. 14th St., and a larger company, William A. Pond & Co. was located at 25 Union Square. Pond's success was due in part to his publication of songs from Harrigan and Hart plays, including the famous *Mulligan Guard* series.

In 1888, a newly created publishing company, M. Witmark & Sons, moved its growing operation from the family home at 402 W. 40th St. to the Rialto. Three years earlier, brothers Isadore, Julius, and Jay Witmark had started the firm, achieving their first success in 1886 with the publication of "President Cleveland's Wedding March."[20] The success generated by the song created the need for larger quarters and the brothers wisely chose to relocate closer to the center of musical activities.

The first Witmark office in the Union Square area was situated in the Demorest building at 32 E. 14th St. which also housed the offices of several women's journals. The constant sounds of the piano in the Witmark's office, however, soon proved incompatible with the quieter activity of publishing ladies' magazines. The brothers were declared public nuisances and, despite holding a one-year lease, were evicted. After a short search, new quarters were found at 841 Broadway, directly across from the Star Theatre, in a building that also housed the Pach Photo Gallery.

When the Witmarks moved to 841 Broadway, Willis Woodward, a competitor with offices in the Star building, predicted: "I'll give those blankety-blank-blank Witmarks just six months in this business."[21] Instead of perishing, however, the Witmarks thrived, with an unbroken string of hit songs which included "The Picture That Is Turned Toward the Wall," "The Wedding of the Lily and the Rose," "I Long to See the Girl I Left Behind," and the immensely popular "Throw Him Down, McCloskey," Maggie Cline's trademark. Among the first to recognize the potential market for popular music, the brothers exploited their show business connections—Julius was a popular performer at Pastor's and Koster and Bial's while Isadore was an established song-plugger—to place their songs with the best variety performers. Tony Pastor's headliners were especially kind to the brothers, and the list of his stars to sing Witmark songs included Joe Hart, Bessie Bonehill, Vesta Victoria, Lottie Gilson, and Eunice Vance.

Representing composers like Victor Herbert and George M. Cohan, the firm quickly outgrew its Broadway office. In 1893, M. Witmark & Sons moved to 49-51 W. 28th St. in the heart of the newly emerging Tin Pan Alley. Situated one block to the west at 109 W. 28th St. was the Arthur W. Tams Circulating Library, with whom the Witmarks would later merge. Shortly after the Witmarks moved to W. 28th St., their former quarters at 841 Broadway were demolished to make way for the Roosevelt building.

Side by side with the larger and more prosperous enterprises like Samuel French & Son and Brentano's, a host of small businessmen made their livings providing goods or services to the theatre or the theatre-going public. William H. Brown on E. 14th St. near 1st Ave., Charles Schultz at the western end of 11 St., and Wetherspoon Brothers at 426 W. 13th St. stocked the lumber needed for sets; while Samuel Martin, 127 8th Ave. near 16th carried a full inventory of theatrical hardware. John Hall's Oddity Shop at 53 W. 18th St. near Chickering Hall sold a wide range of theatrical souvenirs. Seer's Theatrical Printing Shop at 26 Union Square, J. F. Jackson, Theatrical Printer and Engraver, at 12 Union Square, W. L. Hyde and Company at 22 Union Square, and Leo Von Raven, 113 E. 14th St., printed programs for many of the leading theatres, including Tony Pastor's, Daly's Theatre, and Chickering Hall. Nearby, *The Bill of the Play,* a forerunner of today's *Playbill,* was published at 33 Union Square. This elaborate program, which consisted of four pages of biographies, advertisements, and upcoming attractions, in addition to the usual cast list, was furnished to the Fifth Avenue Theatre, the Academy of Music, Steinway Hall, the Eagle Theatre, Robinson Hall, and many of the leading hotels.

Throughout the Union Square area, ticket-selling thrived. Brentano's, Schirmer's, and other book or music dealers sold tickets, acting as extensions of the theatre box offices, while ambitious speculators sold tickets without the theatres' permission, frequently from offices in choice locations. In the mid-seventies, the Bijou Ticket Office at 33 Union Square advertised that it remained open from 7 a.m. to 7 p.m. to provide ''choice seats for all Theatres, Operas, Concerts [and] Lectures.''[22] The Bijou Ticket Office also provided diagrams of the leading halls, as did T. J. McBride, founder of McBride's Theatre Ticket Company, who had begun as a ticket broker in the lobby of the Union Square Hotel. The majority of speculators, however, were little more than ''scalpers'' who hawked tickets outside the theatres before curtain time. While the scalper had been a nuisance for theatre managers as early as 1850, his ranks swelled to the size of a small army by the seventies, and Henry Irving recalled seeing an audience ''mobbed by a band of ticket speculators, with satchels strapped to their shoulders, announcing in hoarse tones, even under the box office windows, 'I have seats in the front. . . . I have the best seats in the orchestra.' ''[23]

Of the entrepreneurs whose livelihood depended upon furnishing either goods or services to the theatre, none reflected the theatre's evolution into big business more than the agent. Before the mid-1870s, both the hiring of actors and the booking of shows was accomplished while actors and managers were "filling time" on the sidewalks near Union Square, an area known to theatre people as the "slave market." There, also, entire companies were engaged for appearances in other cities. Contracts, often verbal or scribbled on scraps of paper, were enacted while the parties sat on a bench in the square or at a table in a nearby restaurant.

Like his twentieth-century counterpart, the nineteenth-century agent was a professional middleman who received a fee for referring an actor to a particular manager or for furnishing a desk where negotiations could take place. The early agents maintained offices near the center of theatrical activities where managers could list their needs, either in person or by letter, and where actors and actresses could post their photos on the wall for a small fee. Prior to 1870, the agencies were little more than clearing houses for talent and often the agent was not involved in the final negotiations between actor and manager. This resulted in frequent complaints from actors, who "charged that even when they negotiated directly with the managers they were frequently compelled to sign agreements at the agencies and to pay . . . for services which were not rendered."[24] Nevertheless, with an estimated 200,000 people in the United States connected with the theatre in 1870 (the majority of them actors), clearing houses for talent were rapidly becoming a necessity for the average actor and a time-saving convenience for the manager.

By the mid-seventies, the hiring of actors had moved indoors from the "slave market" to agents' offices, and the agent's role was on the verge of a major redefinition.[25] When stars began hiring agents to handle their business transactions, often at salaries in excess of $100 per week, the talent broker was immediately placed in a strategic position.[26] He alone decided for whom an important actor would work. Negotiating for the stars concentrated an enormous amount of power in the hands of a few individuals who could control not only the futures of the performers they represented, but the fates of managers throughout the country.

With power, money, and a certain prestige to be gained (often overnight if a major star was represented), scores of enterprising men entered the ranks of New York agents. Between 1875 and 1880, the number of agencies grew rapidly and the agent's domain was expanded to include not only performers, but also scenic artists, stage carpenters, and property men as well. Beginning in 1875, agents were attracted to the Union Square area, and five years later it was unthinkable to establish or attempt to maintain an office below 14th St.

The first agency to move to the Rialto opened in March 1875 at 10 Union Square, adjacent to the *Dramatic Mirror*. The Simmonds and Wall Dramatic Agency had been created in April 1874 from a merger between Horace Wall's Dramatic Agency and Morris Simmond's International Dramatic Agency, two of New York's oldest and most influential theatrical firms. While the merger appeared successful to observers of the time, it was short-lived. In the April 14, 1877, edition of the *Clipper*, Simmonds and Wall announced the dissolution of their partnership for undisclosed reasons. Simmonds remained at 10 Union Square, operating once again as the International Dramatic Agency, while Wall leased an office on the ground floor of the Union Square Hotel where one of his protégés was Maze Edwards, later a successful agent in his own right with offices at 41 Union Square.

Two months after Simmonds and Wall dissolved their partnership, the Brown and Barnes Dramatic Agency was opened at 854 Broadway by J. Alexander Brown and James Barnes. The newcomers represented not only actors on the legitimate stage, but musical, variety, equestrian, and minstrel performers as well. The agency, advertised as being close to the center of dramatic activities, was open seven days a week, with Sunday hours from 10 a.m. to 2 p.m. "for the convenience of all." In 1879, Barnes retired and Brown moved to 64 E. 14th St., on the corner of 4th Ave. next to the Morton House, where he provided rehearsal space for small companies in addition to the agent's routine services. In 1881, he opened a second office at 169 Bowery exclusively for variety artists.

After 1877, others followed the lead of Simmonds, Wall, Brown, and Barnes. In July 1878, R. Fitzgerald and Company's Dramatic, Equestrian and Variety Bureau opened at 63 E. 14th St. and later the same year C. Randolph Gardiner opened the Managers' and Stars' Agency at 12 Union Square. In May of the following year, T. Allston Brown established an office (in partnership with Morris Simmonds) at 863 Broadway. Long one of New York's premier agents, with a background as a manager and theatre historian, Brown at the time represented more than 500 performers, including serio-comic singers, jugglers, musicians, ballet masters, song and dance men, roller skaters, ventriloquists, gymnasts, acrobats, and premiere danseuses. Among the notables he booked were the Worrell Sisters, the Levantine Brothers, Agnes Sutherland, and Marie Bonfanti, as well as *The Two Orphans* combination company. With Brown's list of clients and Simmonds' international interests, the merger created the city's most influential agency.

During the early eighties, the agent's role was changing in a way that would have widespread ramifications and permanently alter the economic structure of the American theatre. Shortly after opening his agency on Union Square, C. R. Gardiner undertook not only to effect agreements between managers and stars, but to gain control over what attractions were booked into what theatres. By controlling the stars' routes himself, instead of letting the individual manager determine the path of a tour, Gardiner was able to force the theatre owner to deal directly with him in order to sign attractions. This principle of "exclusive control over the theatres and attractions, a principle later put into practise by the Klaw and Erlanger Exchange over a limited territory, and still later by the Syndicate over the first-class theatres of the entire country" created an entirely new type of agent— the booking agent.[27]

By the middle eighties, booking was flourishing on 14th St., as established actors' agents (T. Allston Brown, J. Alexander Brown, and Morris Simmonds among them) added booking to their lists of services, and newcomers entered the profession. In 1882 Harry Smart and J. J. Spies bought out Gardiner, continuing his agency at 12 Union Square, and the next year John E. Warner opened a booking agency in two rooms at 23 E. 14th St. In September 1883, Warner rented desk space to H. S. Taylor, and when Warner returned to full-time management in 1884, Taylor purchased the agency.

Under Taylor's aggressive management, the agency, now Taylor's Theatrical Exchange, quickly became influential and prosperous. By 1886, Taylor claimed to represent over 100 first-class theatres in the United States and Canada and was charging both the theatres and the attractions he booked fees ranging from $25 to $250. As part of his operation, "he not only represented a large number of theatres, and placed actors, but he also . . . managed the Anglo-American Attraction Agency which 'protect[ed] and purchase[d] plays, contracts for companies, and arrange[d] appearances in England and America.'"[28]

In 1888, Taylor sold the agency to Marc Klaw and Abraham Erlanger, who had formed a partnership the year before. The contract of sale not only granted Klaw and Erlanger ownership of the country's largest and most influential agency, but also eliminated one of their most feared competitors—Taylor himself. Under the terms of the contract, Taylor agreed to refrain from booking for three years. When he later attempted to regain his former status, he had been greatly outdistanced by Klaw and Erlanger, who had made significant advances toward forming the Syndicate that would monopolize booking early in the twentieth century.

At the same time that Gardiner and Warner were establishing their agencies, pioneers in booking vaudeville were also settling near Union Square. In 1882, James Armstrong, one of the first booking agents to specialize in vaudeville with an entree to "the managers of all the leading theatres," opened an office at 10 Union Square. From his quarters overlooking the square, Armstrong supplied leading acts, not only to the major theatres, but the larger summer amusement parks. In 1885, M. B. Leavitt, another pioneer in variety booking, opened an office nearby, at 149 W. 13th St. The office on 13th St. was the nerve center for Leavitt's growing vaudeville circuits in the west and was the training ground for vaudeville's leading booking agent, William Morris. Morris worked sporadically for Leavitt for two years before serving a more extensive apprenticeship with George Liman, another prominent vaudeville agent.

In the early nineties, Union Square became the nation's vaudeville booking center, as the leading agents moved into the area. George Liman maintained offices at 104 E. 14th St., just west of Irving Place; Clint Wilson and Jo Paige Smith (called the Mephistopheles of agents by his contemporaries because of his frequently unethical methods) booked acts for both the Keith and the Proctor organizations from quarters at 853 Broadway; and William Morris opened his first agency at 102 E. 14th St., where he transacted business with many of vaudeville's most influential men, including Willie Hammerstein, Sylvester Poli, and Percy Williams.

By the beginning of the twentieth century, agencies, like most of the other support businesses, had disappeared from the Union Square area. Many of the older agents had retired, while the remainder had moved to offices near 23rd St. or Times

Square, leaving William Morris virtually alone on 14th St. Union Square began to take on the appearance of a ghost town, and when the United Booking Office and the Syndicate began absorbing the smaller agencies in the first decade of the twentieth century, the era of the independent agent was near its end.

9

Satellite Enterprises

By the middle of the nineteenth century, the tradition of beginning an evening at the theatre with dinner and drinks or ending it with dessert or a nightcap at a nearby restaurant was already firmly established. To satisfy these demands, New York restaurateurs provided the nineteenth-century theatre-goer with a practically infinite variety of choices. Many theatres operated cafés where liquor, coffee, and cigars could be enjoyed before the show or at intermissions, and some even maintained small restaurants in their buildings. The wealthy, bound for or returning from the opera, a concert, or a play, could dine elegantly on a multicourse dinner at one of several Delmonico's, at Taylor's Saloon at 365 Broadway, at Louffre's on Pearl Street, at the Maison Dorée on Union Square, or the dining room of the St. Nicholas Hotel.

The less affluent, who comprised the bulk of New York audiences, could choose from an almost endless selection of restaurants scattered throughout the area, ranging from the cheap to the moderately priced. These included oyster and chop houses, which served oysters, chops, steaks, Welsh rarebits, and similar dishes and catered primarily to an evening crowd—mainly theatre-goers and "men about town." There were also German weinstuben, where a wide selection of the best vintages and ample German cuisine were available at reasonable prices, as well as French or Italian restaurants where dinner and wine cost as little as 35¢. By 1875, each of the various types of restaurant was represented on the Rialto.

Like Rector's, Shanley's, Bustanoby's, and Sardi's in the twentieth century, some establishments near Union Square acquired reputations as theatrical restaurants. Many actively solicited the patronage of performers and the after-theatre crowd by advertising not only in the dailies, but in trade newspapers and theatre programs. Others attracted customers from nearby theatres by the type or quality of food and drink they offered, by a special atmosphere, or by offering the privacy sought by performers. These became professional "hangouts" as their reputations spread through the theatrical grapevine. A few, like the Shakespeare Inn and Browne's Greenroom, were actually started by actors and became a haven for the actors from a particular theatre. All shared one common feature—proximity to the theatres.

The first "theatrical" restaurants near Union Square were opened in the mid-1850s by Italian entrepreneurs who catered to the appetites of Italian singers appearing at the Academy of Music. Shortly after the Academy was erected, Italian table d'hôte was being served at Riccadona's, at 42 Union Square; Buchignani's, on 3rd Ave. near 15th St.; Martinelli's near the Everett House on the north side of the square; and Moretti's on the corner of 3rd Ave. and 14th St. At any of these restaurants, an observant opera-fan might have seen Campanini, Trebelli, Ravelli, or Brignoli during the "bel canto" era at the Academy of Music. Signor Moretti, whose most faithful customers were Mario and Grisi, was the first Italian restaurateur in the area and is credited with introducing Americans to spaghetti, olives, chianti, macaroni, and other Italian delicacies. According to legend, Moretti's dinner was "so generous that no one save an Italian singer on his off night could eat all of it."[1]

On Tuesday, April 8, 1862, the New York dailies announced the opening of a restaurant that, while not strictly a theatrical "hangout," would be inextricably tied to the theatre as long as it remained in the area. Delmonico's, already the favorite restaurant of the city's *haute monde*, opened an uptown branch on the following day in the former Grinnell mansion at the northeast corner of 5th Ave. at 14th St. For the next 14 years, the restaurant would be the site of countless before-theatre dinners and after-theatre parties, attended by the wealthier patrons of the Academy of Music, Wallack's, and Steinway Hall.

At the time the restaurant opened, the elegant and liberal Delmonico cuisine was being served at two other locations downtown: one on William St., and the other on Chambers St. at Broadway. The first Delmonico's had been established at 21-25 William St. in 1827 by John and Peter Delmonico, newly arrived from Switzerland. Having prospered in this venture, the brothers opened a second restaurant at 76 Broad St. in 1832 and invited their nephew, Lorenzo, to join the business.[2] In 1846, they opened the Delmonico Hotel at the corner of Broadway and Morris St., selling it in 1855 to open the Chambers St. branch.

The newest Delmonico's was established in a "three-story building, of brick with marble trim, and was dignified and aristocratic-looking, the roof topped by an array of stately chimneys" (fig. 43).[3] The spaces between the building and the sidewalks of both the 5th Ave. and the 14th St. sides were filled with flowers and shrubbery enclosed by an ornate fence. Inside, the rooms were "spacious and beautifully decorated. There [were] numerous apartments for dining parties, besides the general dinner and breakfast halls. It [had] been furnished, at great expense, completely; including sumptuous dinner services, and all that imperial array."[4]

Delmonico's elegant rooms were ideally suited for social functions. The restaurant was the site of countless masked balls, which were in fashion at the time, and it became the rage for mothers to introduce their daughters to society there. Likewise, when the president of the United States, foreign heads of state, government officials, or international celebrities were in New York, they dined at Delmonico's. During the period that the restaurant was on 14th St., Abraham Lin-

Figure 43. Delmonico's. Northeast corner of 5th Ave. and 14th St.
(Courtesy of The New York Historical Society, New York City)

coln, Ulysses S. Grant, Andrew Johnson, William Seward, Benito Juárez, the Grand Duke Alexis, and Charles Dickens were among those who enjoyed the famous cuisine, while General Winfield Scott lived in rooms above the restaurant.

While the work-a-day actor seldom visited Delmonico's, the theatrical profession was by no means excluded. The restaurant's habitués, in fact, included T. Henry French, John McCullough, and comedian Billy Florence, who nightly mingled with the Jeromes, Aspinwalls, Stuyvesants, Jays, and Morgans. Joseph Jefferson and Harry Montague were occasional visitors. The latter, over dinner with Harry Beckett, Arthur Wallack and Edward Arnott from Lester Wallack's company, and "layman" George McLean, first proposed the idea of the Lambs, the famous actors' club, in Delmonico's Blue Room in December of 1874.

In 1876, realizing that "as New York spreads herself, so must the House of Delmonico dilate," Lorenzo and Charles Delmonico closed the 14th St. restaurant, relocating in an even more elegant establishment at 5th Ave. and 26th St.[5] The following year, the building that had become famous as the fifth home of Delmonico's was demolished to make room for a warehouse.

The opening of Wallack's Theatre in 1861 had brought two more restaurants to the area, Browne's Greenroom and the Shakespeare Inn, both operated by members of Wallack's famous company. The first establishment was opened in January 1863 by George F. Browne, who augmented the $9 per week salary he received for playing dialect roles by maintaining a small chop house at 135 4th Ave., opposite the stage door of Wallack's, where he provided chops, steaks, and ham tongue. In addition to choice meats, Browne offered the best brandies, wines, and cigars while soup or chowder was served free every evening until midnight.

Because of the proprietor's affiliation with Wallack's and the restaurant's proximity to the theatre, Browne's Greenroom quickly became the unofficial gathering place for members of Wallack's company and a handful of select outsiders, one of whom was Maurice Barrymore, a member of Augustin Daly's troupe. In an effort to make his regulars (Barrymore, Dion Boucicault, and Harry Montague among them) feel at home, Browne decorated the walls with more than 200 prints and photos of theatrical and musical celebrities, which he advertised as a "Dramatic Picture Gallery." "In this precinct of sanded floors, old theatrical prints, and Toby jugs, fat, jovial George Browne . . . played no part truer than host," narrating stories of the inner workings of the theatre by "one who knows."[6] When Wallack moved to 30th St. in 1881, Browne's Greenroom followed, reopening on 26th St.

Browne's nearest competitor, the Shakespeare Inn at 833 Broadway, one door from 13th St., was opened in March 1863 by W. H. Norton, another member of Wallack's company. In addition to serving much the same menu as Browne, Norton provided a large selection of daily and weekly newspapers, both foreign and domestic. Unlike the Greenroom, which was an immediate success, the Shakespeare attracted few patrons during its first months. Unable to draw the Wallack contingent away from Browne, Norton enlarged his appeal, advertising for the after-theatre crowd in *The Programme*. Simultaneously, he installed a collection of oil paintings and engravings, thus making a visit both "entertaining and pleasing to the palate." Thereafter, the Shakespeare thrived, soon becoming "a resort of the literary and dramatic men of the day."[7]

Several blocks to the south, at the northeast corner of Broadway and 10th St., stood Fleischmann's Vienna Model Bakery and Fleischmann's Vienna Café and Restaurant (fig. 44), erected in 1876 south of Grace Church. Fleischmann's, which remained open until 12 a.m. to serve the after-theatre crowd, was well known for distributing free bread to the poor every night at midnight during the 1880s. According to eyewitnesses, the contrast of 300 to 350 men waiting in the bread line with the richly dressed men and women returning from the theatre or opera and bound for a late supper or dessert at Fleischmann's, created one of the more interesting pictures of the time.

Fleischmann's Restaurant, located on the first floor of the building, was widely known for the excellence of its Viennese coffee, rolls, Bath buns, and "above all its pink ice cream which was served with three cakes, long, crisp and hollow, about the size of [a] thumb and tied with a pink ribbon."[8] In the summer, tables were spread out "under an awninged and vine-embowered enclosure that extend[ed] out to the sidewalk . . . where guests dine[d] in garden-like surroundings."[9] Under the terms of his lease with Grace Church, which owned the land, Louis Fleischmann agreed not to serve malt or alcoholic beverages on the ground floor of the building or on the sidewalk outside. The absence of liquor, the tantalizing array of ices and pastries, and the restaurant's proximity to A. T. Stewart's mammoth emporium one block away, made the restaurant at Fleischmann's extremely popular with the ladies.

The men were treated equally well in the upstairs café where the finest liquors and cigars were readily available. "In the café was situated [a] round table, called by [critic] James Huneker, the 'philosopher's table' . . . Among those who gathered daily about this board" in the 80s were: Huneker; Emanuel Lederer, an actor with the old Stadt Theatre company; Heinrich Conried, manager of the Irving Place Theatre and later director of the Metropolitan Opera House; Carl Herrmann, the manager of the Thalia Theatre; Fleischmann, who not only operated the café and restaurant, but was one of the more generous of the Thalia's patrons; and Anton Seidl, the famous musical director.[10] The latter was taken fatally ill while dining at the famed table in 1898.

By the early 1880s, a number of other theatrical restaurants were in operation in the area. Maria's on 12th St. near 6th Ave., owned and operated by Maria Del a Prato, attracted a bohemian clientele, which included stars of the stage, opera, and lecture circuit. The restaurant was situated in the basement of a three-story building and "the gloomy, low entrance convey[ed] to the passer-by no hint of the hilarity to be found within."[11] The restaurant itself consisted of one room with a bare floor and several long tables spread with the simplest cloths and china:

Figure 44. Fleischmann's Vienna Model Bakery and Fleischmann's Vienna Café and Restaurant. Northeast corner of Broadway and 10th St.
(Courtesy of the Print Archives, Museum of the City of New York)

On Saturday nights Maria's present[ed] a most formidable array of artists, songwriters, models, newspapermen, and celebrities . . . . Speeches and songs [were] heard, anecdotes told, and a couple of musicians with mandolins in one corner of the rooms dispense[d] their melodies liberally.[12]

Among the entertainers who regularly participated in the Saturday night festivities were Joseph Jefferson, Laurence Hutton, Clara Louise Kellogg, and Paul du Chaillu, originator of a popular lecture on the gorilla.

At 2 Union Square, diagonally across 4th Ave. from the Union Square Theatre, Charlie Collins maintained a small restaurant named the Criterion. Collins advertised his establishment as "The Popular Resort for the Elite of the Profession," attracting a sizable contingent from the Union Square Theatre led by Charles R. Thorne. At 11 a.m. each morning, a crowd of actors gathered at the Criterion for a free lunch consisting of a block of cheese and hard crackers served from a long table in the bar. With their lunch spread before them, "the comedians present made funny falls toward the repast while the tragedians advanced with stately tread, and in an incredibly short space of time, nothing remained of the banquet but the rind of the cheese."[13]

One door to the north, Messrs. Schmitt and Fürhman maintained a restaurant on the ground floor of the Hotel Hungaria, which served liberal amounts of German cuisine for moderate prices. From 7 a.m. until 2 a.m. the next morning, actors seeking a culinary bargain, as well as a rendezvous with their colleagues, flocked to the Hungaria (fig. 38). Schmitt and Fürhman also catered to the after-theatre crowd, advertising in the programs of neighboring theatres: "Parties leaving this theatre should not fail to visit the restaurant of the HOTEL HUNGARIA, No. 4 UNION SQUARE, for Oysters and Refreshments. Also serve an elegant Table d'Hote Dinner for 75 cents, from 5 to 8 p.m."

In 1886, Joe Schmitt left the Hotel Hungaria, rented the building on the northeast corner of 4th Ave. and 14th St. and opened his own hotel and restaurant (figs. 45, 46). Immortalized the following year in Hugh D'Arcy's ballad, "The Face Upon the Barroom Floor," the establishment became known simply as "Joe's Saloon" or "Joe's Place."[14] To the singers from the Academy of Music who stayed there, however, Joe Schmitt's was the "Opera Hotel."

Joe Schmitt's was especially popular with the circus and Wild West show performers, and employees of summer amusement parks who lived near Union Square during the off-season. These showmen gathered daily in Joe's Place and from noon until early the next morning events of the past season, predictions about the coming season, changes in management, and personal news were discussed. Because of the patronage of these "minor" performers, Joe's Saloon remained a theatrical rallying place long after the Rialto had moved to Times Square. In 1921, however, Joe Schmitt's, like the other buildings on the same block, was absorbed by Klein's Department Store.

Of all the restaurants in the area, few had closer ties to the theatre than Lüchow's at 110 E. 14th St. (fig. 47), and many notable actors and musicians could

Figure 45. Joe Schmitt's Hotel and Restaurant. Northeast corner of 4th Ave. and 14th St.
(Courtesy of The New York Historical Society, New York City)

Figure 46.   Interior of Joe Schmitt's Restaurant.
(Courtesy of The New York Historical Society, New York City)

repeat critic James Huneker's claim that, "I took a walk and got as far as Lü-chow's." While Union Square was still the Rialto, Paderewski played at Lüchow's, Fritz Kreisler entertained at a private party in an upstairs room for an entire evening, and Gus Kahn is rumored to have composed "Yes Sir, That's My Baby" on a Lüchow tablecloth.[15] Nightly, such regulars as Lillian Russell (in whose honor a private room was named), O'Henry, Sigmund Romberg, and Victor Herbert were entertained by the Vienna Art Quartet in the upstairs rooms, while Caruso, Richard Strauss, and Dvořák dined at Lüchow's when in New York. The patrons and employees of Steinway Hall met nightly in the Steinway room, just down the hall from the private room reserved for Heinrich Conried and his German actors from the Irving Place Theatre. In the café downstairs, critics wrote their reviews over mugs of beer, and in yet another room on the second floor the famous club, the Bohemians, was organized by Huneker and Rafael Joseffy. At roughly the same time, the Society of Authors and Composers was also founded at Lüchow's.[16]

From the outset, the restaurant had a musical and theatrical ambiance. Opened as one of the many German beer halls in the neighborhood in the late seventies by Baron Otto Von Mühlbach, the original restaurant was only one-eighth of the size of the twentieth-century establishment. From its opening, Von Mühlbach's sumptuous dinners and wide selection of imported beers attracted theatre-goers, and the beer hall was popular with performers working in the area. German singers appearing at the Academy of Music retreated to the baron's after the opera and Tony Pastor routinely took his lunch there, exchanging jokes and gossip with the waiters.

In 1880, Von Mühlbach hired 24-year-old August Lüchow as a waiter and bartender. Under the baron's tutelage, Lüchow learned the restaurant business. When Von Mühlbach retired two years later to return to his native Munich, he sold the restaurant to Lüchow, who combined his savings with a loan from William Steinway to meet the purchase price. Capitalizing upon the contacts and experience gained while working for Von Mühlbach, Lüchow's rise to prominence was meteoric. When Huneker took his famous walk in 1886 and wrote about it the following day, hundreds of people who had never heard of the restaurant "took a walk" to Lüchow's. In 1902, Lüchow received more free publicity when the song, "Down Where the Würtzburger Flows" (written to honor Lüchow) became popular, and a new wave of curiosity-seekers flocked to his café to drink the celebrated draft.[17] By the time August Lüchow died in 1923, the restaurant had been expanded into 106 and 108 E. 14th St. (purchased from Huber in 1910) and employed 120 waiters.

While some people were lured to the restaurant by the opportunity of dining among the stars of the theatrical and musical worlds, most came to sample the legendary cuisine, drink beer, and enjoy Papa Lüchow's hospitality. "There was nothing Broadwayish about Lüchow's. On entering [one] always got a sense of vastness. The center room was very large and open, a sort of closed beer-garden" where the aroma of Würtzburger mixed with the smells of Weiner schnitzel, sauer-

Figure 47.   Lüchow's. 110 E. 14th St.
(*Courtesy of The New York Historical Society, New York City*)

braten, venison, and noodle soup.[18] The inner rooms (fig. 48) with their ''heavy Teutonic décor,'' ran the entire length of the restaurant, from 14th to 13th St., and accommodated hundreds; while the upstairs rooms afforded the maximum in privacy and elegance. Regardless of where one dined, there was a *gemütlichkeit* throughout Lüchow's.[19]

The center of attraction for many, however, was the massive bar where 24,000 seidels (liters) of beer were served daily. During the day, a huge free-lunch counter was set up opposite the bar, being replaced in the evening by an equally impressive pastry counter where five waiters sliced cheesecake. From noon until closing each day, there was nonstop traffic between the bar and the counter. This was the area of the restaurant where Papa Lüchow, a rotund Hanoverian, conducted business with the pride of a maestro. If he knew a customer, even slightly, Lüchow would join him at a table and provide the first round of beers; and everyone, friend and stranger alike, was greeted with a hearty, ''Come, my friends. All are welcome.'' Often, according to veteran waiters, Lüchow overplayed his role of host, partaking of too many rounds with his guests, and four waiters were required to carry him to his apartment above the restaurant.

However, not even the jovial, hospitable Lüchow was prepared to welcome the restaurant's most unusual guest. One evening ''a lion, fattened on scraps from the restaurant's kitchen, had escaped from his cage next door at the Hubert [sic] Museum; barely ambulatory, toothless, he had waddled into Lüchow's dining room in search of leftover dumplings and sausage ends.''[20] On that occasion, Lüchow joined his customers as they fled from the building.

In the spring of 1982, Lüchow's, once called a ''gastronomic cathedral,'' celebrated its centennial on 14th St. The restaurant had survived the northward march of the city, three wars, several depressions and changes in management, as well as two periods of strong anti-German sentiment that led to the bankruptcy of many other German businesses. In June of the same year, however, Lüchow's moved back to the center of theatrical activity, relocating on Broadway opposite the Winter Garden Theatre. Although the original building with some of its décor removed remains and is currently being used as a discotheque, the long-range future of the former Lüchow's remains uncertain.

Like the theatrical restaurants, many hotels near Union Square played a vital role in the daily life of the Rialto. Before apartments became popular and widely available, people who did not own their own homes lived either in boarding houses or in one of the city's hotels.[21] While some hotels of the era catered almost exclusively to visitors, and most reserved a proportion of their rooms for short-term guests, many were regarded as residential hotels. Between 1850 and 1880, the population of New York's hotels would have formed a small city.

In the 1870s, with a growing number of performers eager to board near their places of employment, many of the hotels on or near Union Square gained a distinctly theatrical character. Some were small and relatively short-lived, such as the Monument House at 6 Union Square in the late seventies (fig. 38), and the

Figure 48.   Side Room at Lüchow's.
(Courtesy of The New York Historical Society, New York City)

Irving Hotel on the corner of 14th St. and Irving Place in the late eighties. Others—the Morton House, the Union Square Hotel, and the Everett House—were among the city's largest and best appointed hotels.

One of the largest and most popular theatrical hotels on the square, the Morton House (fig. 49), occupied the entire block between 4th Ave. and Broadway. During the square's Rialto period, the Morton House was home to hundreds of theatre professionals. When Maurice Barrymore and Charles Vandenhoff arrived in New York in 1875, the hotel was their first address; James Huneker's famous walk to Lüchow's in 1886 began at the door to his room in the Morton House; the Irving-Terry company stayed there in 1888 while appearing at the Star Theatre next door; Sheridan Shook, J. M. Hill, and James M. Collier maintained rooms in the hotel while they managed the Union Square Theatre downstairs; and the Morton House appeared frequently as an address in the *New York Mirror Annual and Directory of the Theatrical Profession.* The hotel had a first-class restaurant and café for gentlemen on the ground floor, a Ladies' Dining Room on the second floor, and 200 rooms, each renting for $1.00 per day.

The Morton House originated as the Union Place Hotel in 1848, when a six-story building, built in the middle of the block in the early 1840s, was joined with a new three-story structure to the east. For many years, the original hotel contained the Maison Dorée, a small restaurant that served food equal to Delmonico's. In 1870, Sheridan Shook assumed the lease to the hotel, constructed the Union Square Theatre in the six-story section, and maintained both the hotel, which became the Maison Dorée Hotel during the mid-seventies, and the theatre, until 1881. In that year, the hotel was purchased by James Morton, who changed the name of the establishment and annexed the five-story building to the west of the original complex. With the new addition, the Morton House had 175 ft. of frontage on 14th St. and extended 145 ft. down Broadway.

One of the most popular features of the Morton House was its renowned bar, located in the wing on Broadway. It was "a bar of aristocratic pattern for the nineteenth century, . . . and the players in the city made it a headquarters where searching friends could easily find them."[22] At its small, round tables, important theatrical negotiations were routinely held. Over drinks in 1871, for example, Sheridan Shook and A. M. Palmer formulated the agreement that led to the Union Square Theatre stock company. Shook, Jim Collier, Sheriff O'Brien, and a host of Tammany officials maintained the "amen table" in a corner of the café, where they concocted political schemes years before the famed "Amen Corner" was founded in the Fifth Avenue Hotel.[23]

By the end of the nineteenth century, the Morton House had deteriorated dramatically and had lost its standing in the theatrical community. In 1903, Frank and James Churchill purchased the property, renaming it the Churchill, and maintained it as a second-rate hostelry until its closing in 1923. After the hotel's demise, the Broadway section was demolished, a two-story retail building erected in its

Figure 49. The Morton House. 14th St. Between Broadway and 4th Ave.,
after it had been renamed the Churchill.
(Courtesy of The New York Historical Society, New York City)

place; the first floor of the remaining sections was subdivided and leased for small shops.

Diagonally across the square from the Morton House stood the second major theatrical hotel on the Rialto, the Union Square Hotel (fig. 50). The building had been erected in 1870 on the eastern side of the square by the Brevoort estate and was purchased three years later by Andrew J. Dam and his son, Andrew Jr. The Union Square Hotel, which occupied the lots from 14 to 18 Union Square, elbowed just north of its mid-point to negotiate the bend in 4th Ave. and extended 50 ft. east on 15th St. Standing six stories high, with a sign proclaiming its name extending the entire length of its roof, the hotel dwarfed the smaller buildings to its south, and contained 400 rooms, many occupied by "theatricals."

Shortly after the hotel opened, the café at the Union Square, where two drinks could be purchased for a quarter, became a rendezvous for the theatrical profession. In one corner of the room, a large round table was routinely reserved for Steele MacKaye, Maurice Barrymore, James T. Powers, Lester Wallack, Sheridan Shook, and A. R. Cazuran. "Gathered around a plateau of motley bottles and tall glasses, they sent volleys of shafts and jabs through the blue clouds of Havana-cigar smoke, punctuated by . . . raucous laughter."[24] At a second table in the room, Henry Dazian, J. M. Hill, A. C. Wheeler, McKee Rankin, and Andrew Dam, Jr. met after the theatres closed. The latter speculated in the theatre and advanced money to Henry E. Abbey for a small interest in Sarah Bernhardt's first American tour.

Like the Morton House bar, the Union Square's cozy dining room with its brightly colored table lamps was a common setting for negotiating contracts. According to James T. Powers in his autobiography, *Twinkle Little Star*, a manager willing to pay the price of one of Dam's multicourse dinners could be virtually assured that he would sign a star at half the actor's asking price by the time the dessert was served.

After a series of financial setbacks in the early 1880s, the Dam family lost the hotel in 1885. In the Union Square's remaining years, the management changed several times, during which the hotel was renamed first the Hotel Jefferson and then the Hotel Americana. Finally, in 1921, the property became the northern-most section of Klein's department store, which was razed in May 1984.

The five-story Everett House (fig. 51), named after the orator Edward Everett and erected in 1854 at the northwest corner of 4th Ave. and 17th St., was one of several hotels favored by singers from the Academy of Music. While catering primarily to the stars of the operatic and concert stages, the Everett occasionally hosted representatives from the legitimate theatre. Shortly after James Wallack's death in 1864, many of New York's theatre managers sponsored a luncheon in his memory at the Everett House.

Although primarily a residential hotel (Colonel James Mapleson and Clara Louise Kellogg maintained rooms there), the Everett House reserved a proportion

Figure 50.   The Union Square Hotel. 14-18 Union Square.
(Courtesy of the Print Archives, Museum of the City of New York)

Figure 51. The Everett House. Northwest corner of 4th Ave. and 17th St. (*Courtesy of The New York Historical Society, New York City*)

of its rooms for visiting singers and musicians, who could rent a room for $2.00 per day on the American plan. When the Academy of Music's fortunes declined following the erection of the Metropolitan Opera House, the Everett House deteriorated as well. In 1908, the hotel was razed and the present Everett Building was erected in its place.

On the southeast corner of 18th St. and 4th Ave., the Clarendon Hotel (fig. 52), a large, brick Elizabethan-style building, catered to a wealthy and aristocratic clientele which included the Prince of Wales, the Grand Duke Alexis, Thackeray, Rubinstein, and the leading figures of the concert and lecture circuits. Like the Everett House, the Clarendon was a favorite "abiding place" for the more prosperous members of the operatic community. While the Clarendon offered rooms at $2.50 per day, most of the hotel was composed of suites of apartments rented to long-term tenants. The hotel "was conducted on the American plan and there was a long table in its dining room where whole families ate together in harmony."[25] Unlike the Morton House and the Union Square Hotel, the Clarendon had no bar and what meetings occurred there were held in guests' rooms or in the dining room.

The Westminster, on the corner of 16th St. and Irving Place, was known as "the winter home of literary men" and was Charles Dickens' favorite hotel when he visited New York. Named after the Duke of Westminster, whose coat of arms was etched into the stained-glass windows and printed on the hotel's napkins and stationery, the Westminster was especially popular with English travelers. "The dainty drawing-rooms, . . . [furnished] in the French style; the cream-and-white Colonial dining-room, with its rich-hued curtains, hard-wood floors and rugs; the many commodious guest-rooms [richly] carpeted and furnished . . . [gave] a quiet distinction to this house."[26] During the Rialto period, Christine Nilsson, Denman Thompson, Fanny Davenport, and Annie Pixley were among the stars who maintained apartments at the Westminster.

On the lower fringe of the Rialto, at the southwest corner of 11th St. and Broadway, the St. Denis (fig. 53) was home to Sarah Bernhardt when she visited the city, and housed the uptown branch of the renowned Taylor's Saloon. The hotel's central location and the excellence of the restaurant made the St. Denis particularly desirable for theatre parties.

Opened in 1848, the six-story St. Denis was renovated in 1875 by William Taylor, whose brother ran the famous restaurant on Franklin Street. Following the renovation, the hotel gained a reputation as "one of the handsomest buildings on Broadway" and provided a "quiet and spacious reading-room, dainty parlors, and a Colonial dining-room described as a triumph of refined architecture."[27] Its many public rooms were referred to as being like cozy, pleasant nooks in a refined home. In one of these public rooms, Alexander Graham Bell first demonstrated the telephone on May 11, 1877. During the waning years of the nineteenth century, the St. Denis lost its aristocratic character. Stripped of its ornamentation, the building still stands, opposite Grace Church.

Figure 52. The Clarendon Hotel. Southeast corner of 4th Ave. and 18th St.
(Courtesy of The New York Historical Society, New York City)

Figure 53.   The St. Denis. Southwest corner of Broadway and 11th St.
(Courtesy of The New York Historical Society, New York City)

In addition to providing food, drink, and lodging to the theatrical community, the hotels and restaurants near Union Square furnished meeting space to two professional organizations: the Lambs and the Actors' Fund. The Lambs was founded at Christmas time of 1874 by Harry Montague, Edward Arnott, Harry Beckett, Arthur Wallack, and George H. McLean, a "layman," over dinner at Delmonico's. All were eager to form a supper club that would promote "the social intercourse of members of the dramatic and musical profession with men of the world, and the giving of entertainments for mutual amusement and instruction."[28] After considering possible names for the club, Montague suggested the Lambs, the name of a club in London started in 1869 by John Hare, an eminent British actor. The name of the London club was promptly and unanimously adopted by those present.

During the first year, the Lambs, whose number had grown to seven with the addition of Edward Fox and a Mr. Hurlock early in 1875, held their suppers in various restaurants in the area; at the Maison Dorée Hotel, the Union Square Hotel, and The Matchbox at 848 Broadway, near Wallack's theatre. At these early meetings, "it was decided to increase the membership by 'sevens,' [but] there were so many applications that it was deemed advisable to increase the number to twenty-one."[29]

On May 10, 1877, the club incorporated under the laws of the State of New York. At the time, the membership was just under 60 and included Lester Wallack, Dion Boucicault, Charles F. Coghlan, Billy Florence, E. M. Holland, John McCullough, Eben Plympton, and E. A. Sothern.[30] With its ranks swelling annually, the club quickly outgrew all but the largest rooms in the nearby restaurants and hotels. To alleviate this problem, Montague, as the first shepherd of the Lambs, rented the entire second floor of the Monument House, 6 Union Square, which was converted into a temporary clubhouse.

Following Harry Montague's death in August 1878, Lester Wallack temporarily became shepherd, pending the club's next election. The following year, Harry Beckett, one of the club's founders, was elected to the position. During Wallack's term, the club moved to larger quarters at 19 E. 16th St. With only $80.40 in the treasury, the Lambs were unable to hire outside help and members were forced to transport the club's property personally to the new quarters. This action resulted in some uncomfortable moments for Beckett, who aroused the suspicions of the police and was detained while carrying a portion of the club's pool table across the square.

The Lambs remained on 16th St. until April 1880, when they moved to 34 W. 26th St., the first building to be occupied exclusively by the club. In 1888, while in the 26th St. clubhouse, the Lambs presented the first of their "Gambols" (burlesques written and performed by the members).[31] The show was an immense success, subsequently becoming an annual tradition and one of the trademarks of the club. In 1897, the Lambs moved to a new clubhouse at 70 W. 36th St. and in 1904 they acquired property at 128 W. 44th St. in order to relocate in the heart of the theatre district. Still active, the Lambs currently are located at 3 W. 51st St., in rooms in the Women's National Republican Club.

The theatrical profession's foremost charitable organization, the Actors' Fund of America, was also founded on Union Square by many of the Rialto's most prominent figures. Among the first to realize the need for an actors' fund was Harrison Grey Fiske. As early as 1880, Fiske was using the *Dramatic Mirror* to spur the profession into forming an organization similar to the Shakespeare Lodge of the Actors' Order of Friendship in Philadelphia. Throughout 1881, Fiske's drive for an actors' fund grew in intensity, culminating in an editorial on January 28, 1882, in which "two tragic cases of neglect" were cited and the basic legal and financial structure of a fund was set forth. The editorial evoked a wide-spread response from the profession, including a written offer from Fanny Davenport to give a series of benefit performances. Davenport's letter, dated the same day as Fiske's editorial, was promptly published in the *Mirror* along with the first of several appeals to A. M. Palmer to "start the ball rolling" for the managers.

Even with a possible benefit in the planning stages, Fiske was not satisfied, and on February 18, 1882, he escalated his campaign for a fund by publishing an editorial entitled "A Greek Unburied." In this editorial, Fiske described the case of Eliza Newton, once a prominent actress at the Olympic Theatre, who remained unburied because no funds were available to pay for her funeral. This last editorial paid dividends: Fiske began to receive sizable donations from theatre professionals throughout the country, and on March 2 most of New York's managers met at the Morton House and agreed to donate their box office receipts for April 3 to the fund. One manager, J. H. Haverly, however, was unwilling to wait a full month and donated to the fund the entire proceeds from the March 13 performance of *Sam'l of Posen,* starring M B. Curtis, which was then at the Fourteenth Street Theatre.

In the weeks that followed *Sam'l of Posen* (the first Actors' Fund Benefit), the managers met several times at the Union Square Theatre and at Wallack's to plan for the permanent organization of the fund under the laws of the state, and the scheduled "Actors' Fund Day" was held on April 3 in theatres throughout the city. By June 8, 1882, the day the act of incorporation was passed by the state legislature, the fund had $38,268.16 in its treasury and had dispensed $867.64 for emergency relief.[32] At its first official meeting, held at Wallack's on June 15, Lester Wallack was elected president of the fund; A. M. Palmer was selected as vice-president; Daniel Frohman was voted secretary; and Theodore Moss was chosen to serve as treasurer. At this time, the funds' first headquarters, which featured a library assembled by Brander Matthews and an "actors' exchange" where information on job openings was posted, was established in a room at 12 Union Square, donated by Fiske.

After 100 years, "the primary purpose of the Fund today is, as it was at its inception, the gathering and conserving of money—in order to be able to relieve the financial distress of those in the profession who are destitute."[33] Under the current presidency of Nedda Harrigan Logan, the fund maintains headquarters at 1501 Broadway, as well as a retirement home in Englewood, New Jersey, which currently houses about 50 ex-professionals. In 1982, the fund distributed over $1 million, "not just to actors, but to workers and performers in all areas of entertainment."[34] Its gala "Night of 100 Stars," held at Radio City Music Hall on February 14, 1982, marked the Actors' Fund centennial and raised in excess of $1.5 million. With the proceeds, the Actors' Fund hopes to erect a nursing home on the grounds of the present actors' home. Like the Lambs, Dazian's, the William Morris Agency, and Samuel French, Inc., the Actors' Fund today serves as a living reminder of Union Square's once-glorious past.

10

The Decline of the Rialto

By the beginning of the twentieth century, Union Square had fallen victim to New York's unceasing march northward and had been superseded as the city's Rialto, first by Madison Square, and then by Long Acre Square (renamed Times Square in 1904). In 1900, there was a steadily growing cluster of theatres at Long Acre Square; Tin Pan Alley had settled temporarily on W. 28th St. before becoming more firmly entrenched near the Brill Building on W. 49th St. in 1908; many of the costumers, script sellers, and agents who had prospered near Union Square during its Rialto period, had leased new quarters in the West 40s; and, George Considine's Metropole Bar and Restaurant at the corner of Broadway and 42nd St. had replaced the Morton House Café as the city's principal theatrical rendezvous.

Union Square's demise as the city's Rialto was the result of 20 years of attrition. Even while New York's first theatrical center was at its zenith in the early 1880s, the events that ultimately would be responsible for its decline already were taking place. In 1880, the Metropolitan Concert Hall was erected on Broadway at 41st St., one block from Long Acre Square; the following year, Lester Wallack moved his renowned company to 30th St.; and in 1882, a second theatre, the Casino (at Broadway and 39th St.), invaded the precincts of Long Acre Square. In 1883, when A. M. Palmer left the Union Square Theatre and the Metropolitan Opera House opened in competition with the Academy of Music, Union Square's fate ostensibly had been determined. Two of its most influential and respected figures, Wallack and Palmer, had moved uptown and its largest and most prestigious theatre was involved in a battle for supremacy which it was destined to lose.

Once started, the process of decay and attrition gathered momentum. Bartley Campbell's disastrous management of the Fourteenth Street Theatre in 1885 destroyed that theatre's reputation as a first-class house, and the following year Colonel Mapleson capitulated in his war with the Metropolitan Opera House. When the Academy of Music became a booking house in 1887, the Metropolitan Opera House became by default the city's official home of opera. By the end of the decade, Union Square had also lost its reputation as the country's booking center for the legitimate stage. In 1889, Klaw and Erlanger had moved the former Taylor Exchange, the nucleus of the soon-to-be-formed Theatrical Syndicate, to 23rd St., and many of the other agents followed.

With its foundation gone, the Rialto's collapse was imminent. Between 1890 and 1895, five new theatres—Carnegie Hall (1892), the American Theatre (1893), the Empire Theatre (1893), Abbey's Theatre (1893), and Oscar Hammerstein's mammoth Olympia (1895)—were built near Long Acre Square. Union Square, meanwhile, continued to lose theatres and theatrical businesses. In 1890 William Steinway closed the large concert-lecture room in Steinway Hall, and two years later Chickering Hall ceased operation, Brentano's moved uptown, and Theodore Moss relinquished his lease to the Star. Following Moss' retirement, the Star quickly slipped from the ranks of New York's first-class theatres, subsequently housing burlesque and second-rate combination companies. One year later, in 1893, the area's only remaining first-class dramatic theatre, the Union Square, ceased presenting dramas and became the home of continuous vaudeville under Keith and Albee.

By the end of the nineteenth century, Union Square had relinquished its status as the nation's vaudeville booking center, most of the booking agents having moved north in the late 1890s, and was soon to lose two more respected theatrical businesses and one of its most famous landmarks. In 1900, the Eaves Costume Company moved to W. 46th St., followed the next year by Dazian's, which rented new quarters on W. 44th St. When in May of 1901 New York's daily newspapers announced the closing and demolition of the venerable Star, long identified with the square's golden period, the headlines served as an obituary both for the theatre and for the Rialto as it once had been.

Although by 1900 Union Square finally surrendered its role as New York's theatrical headquarters to Long Acre Square, "the northward march . . . did not close the Old Rialto. [Its] influence was too great to fade in one generation, and despite its faded glories, it still [clung] tenaciously" to a lesser place in the city's entertainment industry.[1] Until 1910, the Academy of Music still presented popular dramas, Keith's and Tony Pastor's theatres remained among the city's premier vaudeville houses, and Huber's Museum continued to show the country's most famous freaks and novelties. Union Square still attracted thousands of amusement-seekers daily, primarily immigrants and laborers who were too timid to journey to the sophisticated "white light district" farther uptown.

Likewise, many of the theatrical hotels and restaurants near the square continued to prosper, despite the absence of their former habitués. The Hotel Hungaria, the Union Square Hotel, Lüchow's, and Joe Schmitt's, once the rendezvous for opera singers and members of the Wallack and Union Square companies, became havens for entertainers from vaudeville and burlesque houses, tent shows, summer amusement parks, Wild West shows, dime museums, penny arcades, and nickelodeons.

The continued success of live entertainment during the first decade of the twentieth century was due in part to two theatres—the Irving Place and the Dewey—opened late in the square's Rialto period.[2] The first (fig. 54) had been erected on the site of the demolished Irving Hall and opened on December 1, 1888, as the Amberg Theatre. Gustave Amberg, the first proprietor of the 1,250-seat house and former manager of the Thalia Theatre, maintained a 120-member stock company and mounted productions of the classics and an occasional opera in German for a predominantly German audience. For four years, Amberg, assisted by Adolph Neuendorff and Leo Von Raven, the theatrical printer, continued to present German language plays, and his theatre became a popular resort for the wealthy German families of 2nd Ave.

In October 1893, Heinrich Conried leased the house, changing its name to the Irving Place Theatre. During his tenancy, the theatre was transformed from the exclusive German establishment run by Amberg into a "centre of intellectual culture for Americans as well as for Germans."[3] Conried's stock company was reputedly one of the best in the city and its collective talents were regularly supplemented by visiting stars from Germany. Under Conried's management, the Irving Place prospered until 1914, when anti-German sentiments, prevalent throughout the United States during the First World War, initiated its decline.

Periodically, between 1914 and 1918, the theatre was used for vaudeville and movies. In the spring of 1918, it was leased by a Yiddish company headed by Maurice Schwartz, a rising young star in the Yiddish theatre, and on September 18, the Irving Place reopened with a production of S. Ansky's *The Dybbuk*. Two years later, following a disagreement with company members, Schwartz left the Irving Place and the theatre's fortunes began once again to decline.

During the 1920s and 1930s, the theatre was known as the Irving Burlesk, joining B. F. Kahn's Union Square Theatre and the Olympic in presenting two-a-day strip shows for an eager public. As its nearest competitors went out of business, the strip acts at the Irving Burlesk grew increasingly more daring and the theatre prospered until License Commissioner Moss banned strip shows in 1937. With burlesque outlawed, Yiddish melodrama returned briefly to the Irving Place in the late thirties and in the forties and fifties the theatre showed art films until it was sold to Klein's for use as a warehouse.

The second theatre, the Dewey, at 126-130 E. 14th St., was built and opened in 1898 by Tim Sullivan, a Tammany politician, and George Kraus. Although the Dewey was advertised as a vaudeville theatre and occasionally presented a bill suitable for the entire family, it was better known as a "wheel" burlesque house catering to all-male audiences. Kraus and Sullivan's major attractions, during the eight years they managed the Dewey, were scores of beautiful girls clad in tights and an uncommonly well-stocked bar in the theatre's basement. In July 1908, Kraus and Sullivan leased the theatre to William Fox who presented a bill that included both vaudeville and movies.

The opening of these theatres, however, could not save live entertainment in the area. The uptown theatres continued to siphon a proportion of the square's audiences and the growing movie industry claimed the remainder. By 1910, Huber and Pastor had discontinued their operations, the Union Square Theatre had been converted into a movie house, the Dewey was showing movies on the same bill with vaudeville, and the Academy of Music had stopped booking plays and soon became a film house.

Figure 54. The Irving Place Theatre.
(*Courtesy of the Billy Rose Theatre Collection, New York Public Library*)

For the first 15 years of the twentieth century, 14th St. was a hot-bed of film activity, temporarily revitalizing the area. Introduced to the commercial possibilities of film by Koster and Bial, Keith, Pastor, and Oscar Hammerstein in the 1890s, imaginative penny arcade operators on 14th St. began installing kinetoscopes and mutoscopes along the walls of their establishments.[4] The kinetoscope, invented by Thomas Edison, and the mutoscope, created and produced by the American Mutoscope Company, were both "peep show" machines that operated on the same principle. The customer inserted a nickel into the machine, looked through a viewing lens, and turned a crank which drew a short (no more than 50 ft.) loop of film past a light source. The result was a moving picture which lasted for a short time, seldom over two minutes.

Among the pioneers in this type of venture were Adolph Zukor and Marcus Loew, both furriers, who jointly established a penny arcade at 48 E. 14th St. in 1903. Unable to attract sufficient patronage with phonographs and other arcade machines, Loew and Zukor added kinetoscopes and mutoscopes to their attractions soon after opening. The "peep show" machines quickly became the arcade's biggest money makers.

Loew and Zukor's arcade (fig. 55) occupied the ground floor of a four-story building two doors west of Broadway, extending from 14th to 13th St. Over an ornate entrance, a giant sign announced the arcade's principal attraction and its price: Automatic Vaudeville for a penny.[5] Inside (fig. 56), rows of machines lined the walls, with mutoscopes and kinetoscopes nearest the front entrance. Over each "peep show" machine, a sign contained a provocative title such as "In My Harem," "Beauty and the Beast," "Peeping Jimmie," or "French High Kickers," and informed the patron about what could be viewed for one penny.

In 1906, Zukor and Loew added projected movies to their operation. By the end of the previous year, with films available on a rental basis, theatres devoted primarily to showing movies had become profitable. Earlier that year, in McKeesport, Pennsylvania, Harry Davis and John P. Harris had established the first successful movie theatre in a vacant store equipped with discarded furnishings from an abandoned opera house.[6] Charging 5¢ admission to their 200-seat theatre, which they called a "Nickelodeon," Davis and Harris realized almost $2,000 in their first two weeks of operation.[7]

Witnessing Davis and Harris' success, ambitious showmen soon realized that anyone who could lease a deserted storefront, buy or borrow a projector, and set up several rows of chairs could become wealthy overnight. By the end of 1906, there were more than 1,000 nickelodeons in the United States (300 in New York alone), and by 1907, 200,000 people per day patronized these primitive movie theatres.[8] Quick to sense the future popularity of the nickelodeon, Zukor and Loew, early in 1906, had rented the first floor of the building adjacent to their arcade (at 46 E. 14 St.), formerly occupied by the Gophir Diamond Company, removed the jewelry display cases, and installed seats, a piano, and a movie projector.

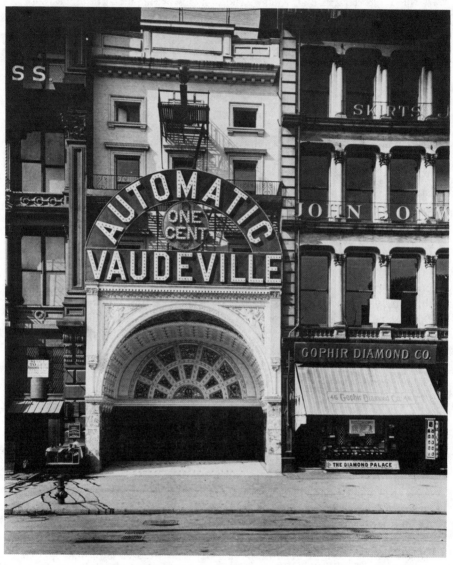

Figure 55.   Entrance to Adolph Zukor and Marcus Loew's Penny Arcade. 48 E. 14th St.
(Courtesy of the Theatre Collection, Museum of the City of New York)

Figure 56. Interior of Zukor and Loew's Penny Arcade. Viewed from the front of the building. A row of mutoscopes may be seen at the left of the picture with kinetoscopes across from them. (*Courtesy of the Theatre Collection, Museum of the City of New York*)

Zukor and Loew's movie house, named the Comedy Theatre (fig. 57) was one of the earliest nickelodeons in the area and launched both proprietors' successful careers in the motion picture industry.

One block to the west of the Comedy Theatre, the former Steck Hall at 11 E. 14th St. housed the offices and studio of the American Mutoscope and Biograph Company. The company had been formed as the K.M.C.D. Syndicate early in 1895 by E. B. Koopman, Henry Norton Marvin, Herman Casler, and William Kennedy Laurie Dickson, a former Edison assistant, in order to create a "peep show" machine that would compete with Edison's kinetoscope.[9] Within months, the partners succeeded in creating a viewing machine called the mutoscope, superior to Edison's and capable of projecting film designed for use in the kinetoscope. Since Edison was the only movie producer in the country at the time, the partners were forced to ask him to supply them with films, a proposition Edison flatly refused.

With an efficient machine for showing moving pictures, but no source of films, K.M.C.D. decided to produce its own movies. By the fall of 1895, Casler had developed an efficient camera and Koopman had created the American Mutoscope Company, which was initially housed at 840 Broadway. Backed by corporate as well as private investments, the American Mutoscope Company was ready to begin filming by the end of the year.[10] One of the company's earliest efforts starred Joseph Jefferson (also an investor in the company), who recreated two scenes from his celebrated stage role of Rip Van Winkle in 1896. The filming of "Rip's Awakening" and "Rip's Toast" on Buzzard's Bay marked the first appearance of a stage star before a movie camera in America.

Capitalizing on the success of the mutoscope, the partners concentrated upon developing their projector, the biograph, changing the firm name to the American Mutoscope and Biograph Company, and moving to larger quarters in the once elegant Cunard mansion, a four-story brownstone at 11 E. 14th St. (fig. 58).[11] At the rear of the first floor, the former Cunard ballroom which had also served as the concert room while the building was known as Steck Hall, had been converted into the company's studio. The 35- by 50-ft. studio (fig. 59) was equipped with Aristo "flaming arc" lamps and Cooper-Hewitt mercury vapor lamps. The room contained stage scenery and there were adjoining dressing rooms. The cutting room, shipping room, and a small projection room were located on the second and third floors, while the fourth floor was reserved as a laboratory for future experimentation. The basement was used as a warehouse for discarded scenery and props.[12]

During the years the company was located on 14th St., Mary Pickford, Mack Sennett, Dorothy and Lillian Gish, Blanche Sweet, and Mabel Normand began their illustrious movie careers with Biograph. The studio's most famous discovery, however, was David Wark Griffith, who was hired in 1907 as an actor and quickly graduated to director. His first film, *The Adventures of Dollie,* opened July 14, 1908, at the Union Square Theatre. By the time Biograph moved to 175th St. in

Figure 57. Zukor and Loew's Comedy Theatre. 46 E. 14th St., adjacent to their penny arcade. The arcade, by this time, had been named Crystal Hall and its name appeared in bas-relief letters over the arcade entrance.

(Courtesy of the Theatre Collection, Museum of the City of New York)

Figure 58. Biograph Studio. 11 E. 14th St.
(Courtesy of The Museum of Modern Art/Film Stills Archive)

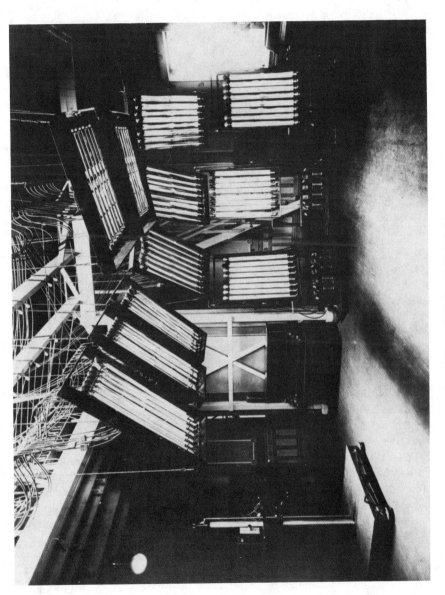

Figure 59. Interior of Biograph Studio. 11 E. 14th St.
(*Courtesy of The Museum of Modern Art/Film Stills Archive*)

1913, Griffith and his cameraman, Billy Bitzer, were revolutionizing movie making and were within two years of making film history with *The Birth of a Nation.*

During the first decade of the twentieth century, 14th St., which was rapidly gaining the reputation as the film industry's "nursery of genius," spawned another motion picture giant: William Fox. In 1906, Fox and Sol Brill, both clothing merchants, had invested $1,000 to lease and equip a penny arcade and nickelodeon in Brooklyn.[13] After six months, Brill withdrew from the venture and Fox, free to set policy and acting upon a friend's advice, instituted a program combining vaudeville acts and moving pictures. On previous combined bills, films were secondary to the vaudeville, being used either as novelties or as "chasers." In Fox's theatre, however, live acts and films were both of the highest quality and shared the bill equally. This policy, dubbed "split pea time" by Keith and F. F. Proctor and later adopted by other managers, brought Fox instant success and became the foundation for an expanding chain of theatres throughout the country.

On July 12, 1908, Fox moved to the former Rialto, leasing the Dewey from Sullivan and Kraus. Although he paid "the largest annual rental known for a theatre not out of the ordinary in size or locale," Fox's "split pea time" formula and his astute management resulted in a profitable venture. Shortly after assuming control of the Dewey, Fox was attracting between 7,000 and 8,000 spectators daily and on one occasion (February 12, 1910), more than 16,000 persons patronized the theatre between 10 a.m. and 11 p.m.[14] With the profits from the Dewey, Fox began acquiring additional theatres in Manhattan and Brooklyn, adding the Gotham and Family theatres in Harlem, the Star Theatre on Lexington Avenue, the Folly Theatre in Brooklyn, and the City Theatre on East 14th St. to his holdings.

The City Theatre (fig. 60), erected early in 1910, at 116 E. 14th St., one door east of Lüchow's, had been financed by Sullivan, Kraus, and a corporation that included William Fox as its principal stockholder. Designed by Thomas Lamb, the 2,500-seat theatre (fig. 61), generally regarded as one of the handsomest in the city, was Sullivan and Kraus' response to rising ticket prices uptown. Their intention in opening the new house was to offer Broadway hits and major stars at prices substantially less than those charged by the theatres around Times Square.[15]

The City Theatre opened auspiciously on April 18, with Anna Held in *Miss Innocence* and a capacity audience "of family parties and young couples, apparently interested in the house as their own place of amusement. In the Lobby were half a dozen floral horseshoes and other emblems of good luck sent to the managers . . . and to Anna Held."[16] The following day, the critics unanimously praised Miss Held's performance, the beauty of the auditorium, and Kraus and Sullivan's daring in building the only English-language legitimate theatre below 28th St. Unfortunately, the opening night was to be the City Theatre's zenith; following the first performance, attendance plummeted, and by December, Kraus and Sullivan had sold their interests in the theatre to Fox, who promptly installed his popular "split pea" programs.

Figure 60. The City Theatre.
(Courtesy of the Theatre Collection, Museum of the City of New York)

Figure 61. Interior of the City Theatre. Shows the private boxes and a portion of the orchestra. *(Courtesy of the Theatre Collection, Museum of the City of New York)*

By the time he assumed full control of the City Theatre, Fox already had become a leading figure in the motion picture industry. His Greater New York Film Rental Company was a major distributor of short program films; he had purchased theatres all over the city; and he had acquired powerful allies including Tim Sullivan. Fox's broad-based operation and his political allies enabled him to remain independent of the Motion Picture Patents Company and to wage a successful war against the Trust and its distributing agency, the General Film Company.[17] In 1914, denied feature-length films by the Trust and unwilling to rely upon free-lance movie makers, Fox joined the ranks of film producers. Within a year, the Fox Film Corporation had already produced several successful movies, including *A Fool There Was,* which introduced Theda Bara to film audiences throughout the country.

Meanwhile, Fox had acquired additional theatres, including the former home of Grand Opera on 14th St. In 1912, he leased the Academy, which had housed cheap melodrama and nickel vaudeville since 1910, and hired Thomas Lamb to refurbish the interior. Once finished, the elegant new interior (fig. 62), redecorated in red, white, and gold, differed markedly from the crude nickelodeons popular just six years earlier and presaged Lamb's later designs for the Loew, Fox, and Rothafel movie palaces of the succeeding decades. Reopened in 1913, the "new" Academy housed both feature-length films and a resident stock company. Within two years, however, the stock company had been disbanded and, until the end of its existence in 1926, the Academy remained a Fox movie house.

Union Square's tenure as a movie center was brief, from 1908—when Griffith began directing for Biograph and William Fox opened his first large theatre, the Dewey—to 1913. During this period of peak activity, with a major film producer located in the area and movies being shown at the Bijou Dream (formerly the Union Square Theatre), the Dewey, the City Theatre, Zukor and Loew's Comedy Theatre, and the Theatre Unique at 136 E. 14th St., the square experienced a renewed vitality. Evidently encouraged by this resurgence, vaudeville impresario B. S. Moss opened a new vaudeville house, the Jefferson Theatre (fig. 63), at 214 E. 14th St. in 1913, and Ben F. Kahn brought his brand of family burlesque to the area the following year, leasing the former Union Square Theatre. For eight years, Kahn maintained the Union Square Theatre as a burlesque house until it was once again converted into a film house, the Acme, in 1922. Moss continued at the Jefferson until 1920, when the theatre became part of B. F. Keith's chain of vaudeville theatres and was renamed B. F. Keith's Jefferson Theatre. In 1932, like the Union Square Theatre before it, the theatre became a movie house called the RKO Jefferson. Abandoned by RKO in the early 1960s, the Jefferson today stands vacant on East 14th St., its façade and marquee still intact.

During the second decade of the new century, the movie industry followed the legitimate theatre and vaudeville north, abandoning the old Rialto. In 1912, Mack Sennett left Biograph to start Keystone Pictures and Adolph Zukor abandoned his downtown interests to form Famous Players. The following year, Biograph left Union Square for larger quarters in the Bronx, and Marcus Loew,

Figure 62. Promenade of William Fox's Academy of Music. Redecorated by Thomas Lamb. (Courtesy of the Billy Rose Theatre Collection, New York Public Library)

Figure 63.   The Jefferson Theatre.
(Author's Collection)

who already had his offices in the Putnam Building on Times Square, installed movies in the Herald Square Theatre. Later in 1913, S. L. "Roxy" Rothafel opened his first New York movie house, the Regent, on 116th St. and ushered in the era of the movie palace. By early 1915, he had leased the Strand Theatre on 47th St. and had brought "the most spectacular entertainment New York had ever seen in a movie house" to Times Square.[18] Rothafel's innovations set the standard for later movie houses: a large tuxedo-clad orchestra seated on stage rather than in the orchestra pit, a corps of uniformed ushers, placement of the projection booth on the orchestra floor resulting in a better image on the screen, and an opulent environment throughout the entire theatre complex.

By 1920, the dark, dingy theatres on 14th St., originally designed for stage shows and later converted into film houses, offered nothing to the movie-goer who had seen the mammoth, opulent movie palaces uptown. Since the demand for movies was sufficient to support both the small film houses and the grand movie palaces, most of the theatres near Union Square remained open as neighborhood theatres. The earlier vitality, however, had disappeared—this time forever. There was a brief rally in 1926 when William Fox built the second Academy of Music at 126 E. 14th St. (now the Palladium) to replace the original Academy, Eva LeGallienne moved her newly formed Civic Repertory Theatre company into the old Fourteenth Street Theatre, and Maurice Schwartz erected the Yiddish Art Theatre at the corner of 12th St. and 2nd Ave. (now the Entermedia Theatre). But by the late 1920s, Union Square had become insignificant in the city's entertainment industry.

During the succeeding decades, the square became a popular site for day-time rallies by unions and local radical groups, and was crowded between 10 a.m. and 5 p.m. with shoppers eager to buy low-priced clothing at Klein's and other area discount stores. At night, however, Union Square took on the appearance of a ghost town. In the words of Robert Grau, who was familiar with the area in its waning years:

> there is nothing about this locale today to remind one of the [old] glories . . . It is enough to make one who has gazed upon the spectacle of other days shudder to find himself in the gloom and desertation which prevails here after dark, where, and it does not seem so long ago, once was the most brilliantly lighted and the gayest spot to be found in the big city—a veritable 'Rialto,' as I recall it![19]

Appendix

Maps of the Union Square District

East of Union Square

1. The Clarendon Hotel

2. Riccadona's, 42 Union Square

3. Dazian's Theatrical Emporium and Seer's Theatrical Print Shop, 26 Union Square

4. W. L. Hyde, printer, 22 Union Square

5. The Union Square Hotel

6. *The Dramatic Mirror;* Nestrock, Theatrical Shoes; J. F. Jackson, printer; and The Managers' and Stars' Agency, 12 Union Square

7. James Armstrong, agent; Charles Winkelmann, wigmaker; and The Simmonds and Wall Dramatic Agency, 10 Union Square

8. A. Roemer & Son, Theatrical Costumes, 8 Union Square

9. The Monument House, 6 Union Square

10. The Hotel Hungaria, 4 Union Square

11. The Criterion and the Koehler Costume Company, 2 Union Square

12. Joe Schmitt's Hotel and Restaurant

13. Steinway Hall

14. The Irving Hotel

15. Irving Hall (later the Irving Place Theatre)

16. The Westminster Hotel

17. The Academy of Music

18. Tammany Hall and Tony Pastor's New Fourteenth Street Theatre

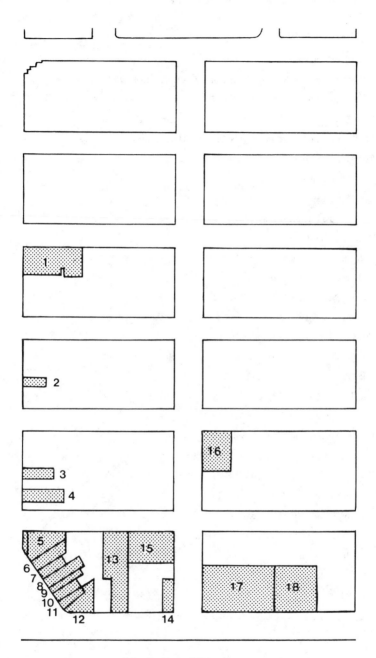

Map I. East of Union Square

South of Fourteenth Street

1. Samuel French and Son, 38 E. 14th St.

2. Zukor and Loew's Comedy Theatre and *The Stage,* 46 E. 14th St.

3. Zukor and Loew's penny arcade, 48 E. 14th St.

4. Clint Wilson and Jo Paige Smith, agents, 853 Broadway

5. M. Witmark and Sons and Pach's Gallery, 841 Broadway

6. The Morton House

7. The Union Square Theatre

8. The Morton House

9. J. Alexander Brown, agent, 64 E. 14th St.

10. Wallack's Theatre

11. William Morris, agent, 102 E. 14th St.

12. George Liman, agent, 104 E. 14th St.

13. Huber's Museum, 106-108 E. 14th St.

14. Lüchow's, 110 E. 14th St.

15. The City Theatre, 116 E. 14th St.

16. The (second) Academy of Music, 126 E. 14th St.

17. The Dewey Theatre, 130 E. 14th St.

18. The Theatre Unique, 136 E. 14th St.

19. Brown's Greenroom, 135 4th Ave.

20. Charles Meyer, wigmaker, 123 4th Ave.

21. The Eaves Costume Company, 63 E. 12th St.

22. The Shakespeare Inn, 833 Broadway

23. *Dramatic Magazine,* 816 Broadway

24. Dodworth Hall, 806-808 Broadway

25. Fleischmann's Vienna Café and Restaurant

26. Bunnell's Museum

27. The Hotel St. Denis

28. Christern's, 77 University Place

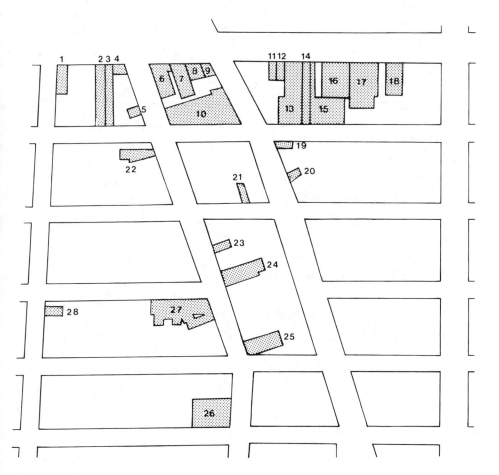

Map II. South of Fourteenth Street

West of Union Square

1. *Freund's Music and Drama,* 30 E. 14th St.

2. Delmonico's

3. Biograph Studio, 11 E. 14th St.

4. Taylor's Theatrical Exchange, 23 E. 14th St.

5. *The Musical Courier,* 25 E. 14th St.

6. The Church of the Puritans

7. William A. Pond & Co., 25 Union Square

8. Schuberth and Company, 27 Union Square

9. Robinson Hall, 18 E. 16th St.

10. Brentano's Literary Emporium, the *Bill of the Play,* and the Bijou Ticket Office, 33 Union Square

11. Gustave Schirmer, Importer of Music, 35 Union Square

12. Napoleon Sarony, 37 Union Square

13. Maze Edwards, agent, 41 Union Square

14. T. Allston Brown, agent, 863 Broadway

15. Andrew Jordan, photographer, 867-869 Broadway

16. Ben Rose, costumer, 872 Broadway

17. Jacoby & Co., costumers, 868 Broadway

18. *The Dramatic News,* 866 Broadway

19. *The Dramatic Times,* 860 Broadway

20. The Everett House

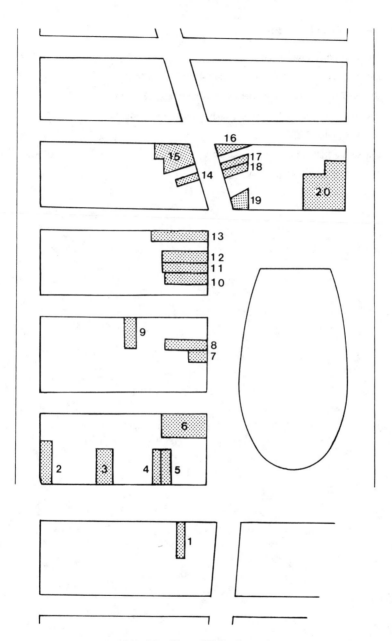

Map III. West of Union Square

The West Fourteenth Street Area

1. The Fourteenth Street Theatre

2. Bloom's Theatrical Supplies Emporium, 48-50 E. 14th St.

3. Charles Eisenmann and Carl Hecker, photographers, 18 E. 14th St.

4. The Bogardus and Feinberg photography studios, 16 E. 14th St.

5. Meade's Midget Hall

6. Chickering Hall, 130 5th Ave.

7. John Hall's Oddity Shop, 53 W. 18th St.

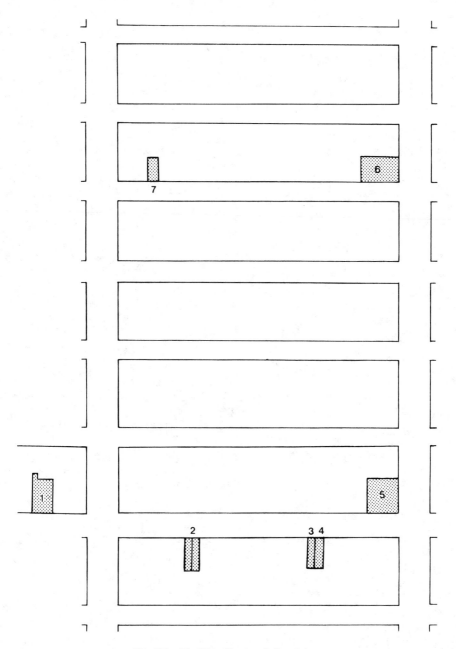

Map IV. The West Fourteenth Street Area

Notes

Chapter 1

1. Mary C. Henderson, *The City and the Theatre* (Clifton, N.J.: James T. White & Company, 1973), p. 139.

2. Barnard Hewitt, *Theatre U.S.A.* (New York: McGraw-Hill Book Company, 1959), pp. 88-160.

3. Henderson, *The City and the Theatre,* p. 50.

4. Bayrd Still, *Mirror for Gotham* (New York: New York University Press, 1956), pp. 129, 205.

5. Foster Rhea Dulles, *America Learns to Play* (New York: D. Appleton-Century Company, 1940), p. 84.

6. Ibid., p. 92.

7. Henderson, *The City and the Theatre,* pp. 103-8.

8. Ibid. Mechanic's Hall (which housed Christy's Minstrels), Wood's Minstrel Hall, and Buckley's Hall (home of Buckley's Serenaders) were the most famous minstrel halls in this area. Not all of New York's theatres in the early 1860s, however, were located in this 10-block section. The Bowery and other theatres remained downtown, while the Academy of Music and Wallack's second theatre were built near Union Square. The erection of the Academy and Wallack's many blocks to the north of the main cluster of theatres served not only as a harbinger of New York's first Rialto, but illustrated the unceasing northward movement of theatrical activity (a phenomenon labeled "The Shifting Rialto" by some historians) that would continue until Times Square became the city's theatrical center early in the twentieth century.

9. Detailed accounts of this transformation and its ramifications are provided by Alfred L. Bernheim in *The Business of the Theatre: An Economic History of the American Theatre, 1750-1932,* and Jack Poggi, *Theatre in America: The Impact of Economic Forces, 1870-1967.* Both trace the economic development of the American theatre from the first signs of the stock system's decay through the domination of the theatre by businessmen like Marc Klaw, Abe Erlanger, B. F. Keith, Edward Albee, and the Shubert Brothers.

10. Alfred L. Bernheim, *The Business of the Theatre: An Economic History of the American Theatre, 1750-1932* (New York: Benjamin Blom, Inc., 1932), p. 26.

11. Susan Lyman, "100 New York Years" (n.p., 1948).

12. Newspaper clipping, "Historic Union Square Marks its 100th Year," n.d., New York Public Library.

13. *New York Illustrated* (New York: D. Appleton & Co., 1869), p. 18.

14. Henry Hope Reed, "The Old Rialto," *New York Herald Tribune,* 19 August 1962, p. 2.

15. Joseph Jefferson, *The Autobiography of Joseph Jefferson,* ed. Alan S. Downer (Cambridge, Mass.: The Belknap Press of Harvard University, 1964), pp. 250-52.

16. Frank Bergan Kelley, *Historical Guide to the City of New York* (New York: Frederick A. Stokes Company, 1909), p. 107.

17. David E. Cronin, "Union Square," unpublished manuscript, New York Historical Society.

18. The concert-lecture hall is defined and discussed in chapter 5.

19. "Street Changes: Concentration of Retail Trades at Union Square," *New York Times,* 21 November 1867.

Chapter 2

1. "The Academy of Music," *Evening Post,* 2 February 1887.

2. *New York Post,* 2 October 1854.

3. Molyneaux St. John, newspaper clipping, "New York Theatres," n.d., Billy Rose Theatre Collection, New York Public Library.

4. For some unknown reason, many drawings of the interior in newspapers of the time erroneously show only 12 boxes instead of the 18 described in written accounts of the theatre. The same drawings invariably fail to show the correct number of Shakespeare boxes, described later in the chapter. With these exceptions, drawings agree with written descriptions.

5. *New York Times,* 3 October 1854.

6. Ibid.

7. St. John, "New York Theatres."

8. Walt Whitman, *New York Dissected* (New York: Rufus Rockwell Wilson, Inc., 1936), p. 21.

9. *New York Times,* 3 October 1854.

10. Julius Cahn, *Julius Cahn's Official Theatrical Guide* (New York: Publication Office, Empire Theatre Building, 1900), p. 23; and *New York Times,* 3 October 1854. In the 19th-century theatre, entrances were made between sets of wings. Thus, each entrance could be designated by a number, beginning at the front of the stage and progressing consecutively to the rear.

11. *Souvenir Book with the Program of the Ceremonies Attending the Closing of the Academy of Music,* May 17, 1926.

12. Ibid.

13. "The Academy of Music," *Evening Post,* 2 February 1887; and newspaper articles, 1864-1879, relating to New York City History, New York Public Library.

14. Henry Edward Krehbiel, *Chapters of Opera* (New York: Henry Holt and Company, 1908), pp. 65-66.

15. Ibid., p. 66.

16. *New York Herald,* 25 November 1859.

17. *New York Tribune,* 28 November 1859.

18. "The Academy of Music," *New York Dramatic Mirror,* 18 June 1910.

19. Allen Churchill, *The Upper Crust* (Englewood Cliffs, N.J.: Prentice-Hall, Inc., 1970), pp. 62-63.

20. T. Allston Brown, *A History of the New York Stage: From the First Performance in 1732 to 1901* (reissued; New York: Benjamin Blom, 1963), II, 51.

21. "The Academy of Music," *Evening Post,* 2 February 1887.

22. Glenn Hughes, *A History of the American Theatre* (New York: Samuel French, 1951), p. 200.

23. Maxwell F. Marcuse, *This Was New York* (New York: LIM Press, 1969), p. 197.

24. According to an undated letter in the Theatre Collection of the Museum of the City of New York from the Academy's Board of Directors to Mapleson, the trustees were aware of the threat to the Academy's position, but failed to take it seriously. They believed that the new corporation would fail to meet its subscription quota and that the dissidents would return to the Academy's ranks.

25. Newspaper clipping, n.d., Billy Rose Theatre Collection, New York Public Library.

Chapter 3

1. "How the Curtain Fell Forever on the Fine Old Star," *Evening Sun,* 22 April 1901.

2. Molyneaux St. John, "New York Theatres," *Broadway,* September 1867-August 1868, pp. 473-79.

3. Ibid.

4. Newspaper Clipping, "Mr. Wallack's New Theatre," n.d., Billy Rose Theatre Collection, New York Public Library.

5. Lloyd Morris, *Incredible New York* (New York: Random House, 1951), p. 65.

6. Clipping, "Mr. Wallack's New Theatre."

7. Cahn, *Theatrical Guide,* 1900, p. 49; and clipping, "Mr. Wallack's New Theatre."

8. *New York Tribune,* 25 September 1861.

9. Newspaper clipping, "Famous Star Theatre is to be Torn Down," n.d., Billy Rose Theatre Collection, New York Public Library.

10. Cecil Derwent Jones, Jr., "The Policies and Practices of Wallack's Theatre," (Ph.D. dissertation, University of Illinois, 1959), p. 80.

11. "The Passing of the Star Theatre," *Evening Sun,* 23 December 1899.

12. Ibid.

13. Newspaper clipping, "The Last of Wallack's," 18 May 1901, Harvard Theatre Collection.

14. The demolition was filmed by the American Mutoscope and Biograph Company and the 50-ft. documentary is available from the Library of Congress Paper Print Collection.

15. Pat M. Ryan, Jr., "A. M. Palmer, Producer: A Study of Management, Dramaturgy, and Stagecraft in the American Theatre, 1872-96" (Ph.D. dissertation, Yale University, 1959), p. 8.

16. *New York Herald,* 13 September 1871.

17. Ibid.

18. *New York Tribune,*12 September 1871.

19. Ryan, "A. M. Palmer," pp. 8-9.

20. Ibid.; and Cahn, *Theatrical Guide,* 1912, p. 409.

21. Union Square Theatre Souvenir Program of the One Hundredth Performance of *Rose Michel.*

22. Ryan, "A. M. Palmer," p. 11.

23. Newspaper clipping, "Happy Days of Palmer are Recalled," 12 September 1915, Harvard Theatre Collection.

24. Ryan, "A. M. Palmer," pp. 30-42.

25. "Boston Manager in New York," *Boston Herald,* 18 September 1893.

26. *New York Times,* 26 June 1896.

27. The balcony and dressing rooms of the theatre had been walled off from the rest of the structure in 1921 to prevent vagrants from entering the building at will. The walls were not totally successful. In 1964, when installing a sprinkler system, workmen discovered the skeleton of a derelict who had used the abandoned theatre as a home.

Chapter 4

1. Thelma Chandler, "Summary of reviews of the Fourteenth Street Theatre's opening night," unpublished paper, Theatre Collection, Museum of the City of New York.

2. Mr. Brecher, critic for the *New York Herald,* cited in Chandler.

3. The remaining seats were situated in eight proscenium boxes which held twelve to fifteen persons each.

4. Cahn, *Theatrical Guide,* 1900, p. 27.

5. Mollie B. Steinberg, *The History of the Fourteenth Street Theatre* (New York: The Dial Press, 1931), p. 35.

6. George C. D. Odell, *Annals of the New York Stage* (New York: Columbia University Press, 1927-1941), X, 254.

7. Brown, *History of the New York Stage,* II, 447.

8. J. Brooks Atkinson, "Art in Fourteenth Street," *Civic Repertory Magazine* 1 (November 1930): 4.

9. Eva LeGallienne, *At 33* (New York: Longmans, Green & Co., 1940), p. 16.

10. Fremont Rider, *Rider's New York City: A Guidebook for Travellers,* 2nd ed. (New York: The Macmillan Company, 1924), p. 295.

11. Odell, *Annals,* VIII, 506.

12. *New York Times,* 3 January 1869.

13. Ibid. The review fails to mention seating capacity, but considering both the size of the top floor at Tammany Hall (approximately 14,000 sq. ft.) and the capacities of other first-class theatres at the time, Jarrett and Palmer's main hall most likely could accommodate between 1,200 and 1,500 spectators. There is no further explanation of the seating.

14. Odell, *Annals,* VIII, 507.

15. Ibid., 507-9.

16. Parker Zellers, *Tony Pastor: Dean of the Vaudeville Stage* (Ypsilanti, Michigan: Eastern Michigan University Press, 1971), p. 70.

17. Ibid.

18. Douglas Gilbert, *American Vaudeville, Its Life and Times.* (New York: Dover Publications, Inc., 1940), p. 10.

19. There is evidence to indicate that Pastor created many of the policies associated with his Fourteenth Street Theatre while he was still downtown. He referred to his first theatre at 201 Bowery as a "family resort"; newspaper ads from Pastor's earliest days as a manager stressed the absence of objectionable material on his bills; and his gimmicks to attract the ladies to his theatre were a common practice while he was at 585 Broadway (1875-1881).

20. Myron Matlaw, "Pastor and his Flock," *Theatre Arts* (August 1958): 20.

21. Odell, *Annals,* XI, 526-28.

22. Montrose Moses, newspaper clipping, "Tony Pastor: Father of Vaudeville," n.d., Billy Rose Theatre Collection, New York Public Library.

Chapter 5

1. The concert hall that presented vocal and instrumental music (usually classical) for an audience of both men and women should not be confused with the concert saloon, also popular at the middle of the nineteenth century. The latter was little more than a smoke-filled beer hall with enticing "waiter girls" and variety entertainment, generally risqué, intended to please an all-male audience.

2. Frank Weitenkampf, *Manhattan Kaleidoscope* (New York: Charles Scribner's Sons, 1947), p. 263.

3. *New York Tribune,* 3 October 1854.

4. Odell, *Annals,* VII, 191.

5. Newspaper clipping, n.d., Harvard Theatre Collection.

6. Ibid.

7. *New York Clipper,* 14 November 1868.

8. While figure 22 shows what appears to be a stage at the far end of the hall, reviews place the performer either at one end of the floor or in the center of the floor surrounded by the audience. With its gallery and private boxes but no stage, Irving Hall was an intermediate step between the concert room and full-scale theatres like Steinway and Chickering Halls.

9. Odell, *Annals,* VII, 366.

10. While the term "stereopticon" was applied to several different projection devices during the nineteenth century, Fallon's Stereopticon appears to have consisted of two lanterns with the capability of allowing one scene to dissolve into the next. According to reviews, the lanterns were also capable of producing images that appeared three-dimensional.

11. *The Programme,* 3 June 1863.

12. Although neither Odell, T. Allston Brown, nor reviews of the time describe a stage, either permanent or temporary, it seems unlikely that a performer like Hartz the Magician could have appeared

before an audience of 1,000, most of whom were seated on a flat floor, without being elevated in some way. Presumably, Irving Hall employed a temporary, raised platform for performances requiring the entertainer to be seen clearly.

13. *New York Clipper,* 15 September 1877 and 1 December 1877.

14. A brief history of the Irving Place Theatre is provided in chapter 10.

15. Robert Grau, *The Businessman in the Amusement World* (New York: Broadway Publishing Company, 1910), p. 16.

16. *New York Tribune,* 10 December 1867.

17. Newspaper clipping, n.d., Harvard Theatre Collection.

18. Newspaper clipping, "Old Steinway, a Landmark Passes," n.d., Theatre Collection, Museum of the City of New York.

19. Weitenkampf, *Kaleidoscope,* p. 264.

20. Ibid., p. 214.

21. Henry Collins Brown, *Brownstone Fronts and Saratoga Trunks* (New York: E. P. Dutton & Co., Inc., 1935), pp. 260-61.

22. Newspaper clipping, n.d., Harvard Theatre Collection.

23. Newspaper clipping, n.d., Harvard Theatre Collection. After the Civil War, there were several groups of former slaves billed as Jubilee Singers. The program of 12 February 1880 does not indicate which group appeared at Chickering Hall.

Chapter 6

1. Odell, *Annals,* V, 486-88.

2. Ibid., VI, 82, 178, 263. Cosmorama was simply another term for a panorama of different parts of the world (cosmos). The diorama was "a form of optical entertainment originally referring to an illuminated show presented in a specifically designed building introduced by Louis Daguerre and Charles-Marie Bouton in France and England in the 1820s. In America, the diorama was largely diluted to mean an elaboration of a panorama devised to show distant views on a painted canvas that rolled from one cylinder to another at the back of a stage." Don B. Wilmeth, *The Language of American Popular Entertainment* (Westport, Conn.: Greenwood Press, 1981), p. 74.

3. Thomas M. Garrett, "A History of Pleasure Gardens in New York City, 1700-1865" (Ph.D. dissertation, New York University, 1978), p. 572.

4. Ibid., p. 579.

5. Newspaper clippings, "The Union Square of Old," and "Evolution of Union Square," n.d., New York Public Library.

6. Garrett, "Pleasure Gardens," p. 579; and *New York Herald,* 3 November 1858.

7. Garrett, "Pleasure Gardens," p. 580.

8. Ibid., pp. 582-83; and *New York Herald,* 13 July 1859.

9. Garrett, "Pleasure Gardens," p. 591.

10. Advertisement, *Dispatch,* 12 February 1865.

11. While figure 30, the only extant rendering of the interior of the Hippotheatron, conveys a general impression of the structure, it is badly scaled, and spatially inaccurate. The advertising for the theatre, for example, indicates that the bandstand (above the entrance to the ring on the right of the picture) was the dividing line between the 50ᶜ and 25ᶜ seats, a fact not reflected in the drawing, and that the two entrances to the ring were directly opposite each other.

12. Program for the Hippotheatron, 26 December, 1864, Theatre Collection, Museum of the City of New York.

13. Program for the New York Circus, n.d., Theatre Collection, Museum of the City of New York.

14. Ibid.

15. Newspaper clipping, n.d., Harvard Theatre Collection.

16. Ibid.

17. Weitenkampf, *Kaleidoscope,* pp. 29-30.

18. Ibid.

19. Frederick Van Wyck, *Recollections of an Old New Yorker* (New York: Liveright, Inc., 1932), p. 130.

20. Newspaper clipping, "Famous Star Theatre to be Torn Down," n.d., Billy Rose Theatre Collection, New York Public Library.

Chapter 7

1. There were two principal reasons for the decline of pleasure gardens by mid-century. First, land in Manhattan was becoming increasingly scarce and prices were skyrocketing, making the cost of a large plot required for a pleasure garden prohibitive. Second, competition from other amusement spots, most notably minstrel halls and variety houses, was siphoning audiences from the pleasure gardens.

2. Since both Robinson Hall and the Columbia Opera House (discussed later in this chapter) were ignored by the critics and diarists of the period, no descriptions of the theatres were recorded. Furthermore, programs, while documenting the nature of the bills presented and recording the names of the artists who performed in these theatres, fail to provide seating charts or fire exits.

3. Newspaper clipping, n.d., Billy Rose Theatre Collection, New York Public Library.

4. Odell, *Annals,* IX, 477.

5. *New York Clipper,* 30 October 1876, 20 May 1876, 10 June 1876, and 8 July 1876.

6. Newspaper clipping, n.d., Billy Rose Theatre Collection, New York Public Library.

7. Michael Leavitt, *Fifty Years in Theatrical Management* (New York: Broadway Publishing Co., 1912), pp. 389-90. Unfortunately, with neither reviews of the sketch nor an extant script, it is impossible to assess the validity of Leavitt's accusation. It is interesting to note, however, that Thompson appeared as a rube in a sketch also titled "The Female Bathers" at the Columbia Opera House in 1876.

8. *New York Clipper,* 19 May 1877.

9. Newspaper advertisement, n.d., Harvard Theatre Collection.

10. James L. Ford, "Movies Where our Rural Drama was Born," *The Evening Post Magazine,* 3 April 1920, p. 5.

11. Ibid., pp. 4-6.

12. *New York Clipper,* 27 October 1877.

13. Obituary of George B. Bunnell, *New York Clipper,* 13 May 1911.

14. It is generally believed that the 10ᶜ admission principle was devised by Charles A. Braden-burgh, a Philadelphia museum operator, but by the time Bradenburgh instituted this price, Bun-nell had been charging a dime for his attractions at his first Bowery museum for several years.

15. *New York Clipper,* 18 December 1880.

16. Newspaper clipping, n.d., Harvard Theatre Collection; and Odell, *Annals,* XII, 139.

17. Advertisement, Worth's Palace Museum, 25 July 1888.

18. Newspaper clipping, 7 January 1889, Harvard Theatre Collection.

19. Advertisement, Worth's Palace Museum, 25 July 1888.

20. Odell, *Annals,* XIV, 389. While accounts of Huber's, at the time, fail to specify the location of the Auditorium Annex, it most likely was on the ground floor, since all of the original curio halls are mentioned in later reports; the second floor theatre continued in operation for several months after the new hall opened; and the top floor still housed performers.

21. "Huber's Museum in the Discard," *New York Telegraph,* 17 July 1910.

22. Brown, *History of the New York Stage,* II, 547. While Brown is specific about the cost of the electrical installation, he mentions nothing of its nature or use.

23. Henry Collins Brown, ed., *Valentine's Manual of Old New York* (Various Publishers, 1916-28), X, 193.

24. *New York Amusement Gazette,* 7 January 1888, 20 February 1888, and 24 December 1888.

25. Ibid., 5 March 1888.

26. Brown, *History of the New York Stage,* II, 547.

Chapter 8

1. "A Dramatic Center," *New York World,* 12 April 1878.

2. *New York Clipper,* 26 April 1879; and *New York Dramatic Mirror,* 25 December 1886.

3. Newspaper clipping, "Costume House is a century old," n.d., Billy Rose Theatre Collection, New York Public Library.

4. *New York Dramatic Mirror,* 25 December 1886.

5. *New York Clipper,* January-April 1881. Anatomical symmetricals, commonly called symmetricals, were pads that ensured that an actor's or actress's curves were distributed evenly on both sides of the body.

6. Carol Webb, newspaper clipping, "A Century in the Theatre," 1943, Billy Rose Theatre Col-lection, New York Public Library.

7. *Wilson's Business Directory of New York City* (New York: The Trow City Directory Company, 1870-90); and *Trow's New York City Directory* (New York: The Trow City Directory Com-pany, 1870-90).

8. Ben L. Bassham, *The Theatrical Photographs of Napoleon Sarony* (Kent, Ohio: The Kent State University Press, 1978), p.2.

9. Ibid., p. 4.

10. Ibid., p. 13.

11. Ibid., pp. 13-14.

12. Newspaper clipping, n.d., Billy Rose Theatre Collection, New York Public Library.

13. The name of the paper was changed to the *New York Dramatic Mirror* on 26 January 1889. It subsequently was renamed the *Dramatic Mirror* on 17 February 1917, the *Dramatic Mirror and Theatre World* on 16 October 1920 (after absorbing *Theatre World*), and *The New York Mirror* on 12 December 1921.

14. Marcuse, *This Was New York*, p. 227.

15. Before the transatlantic cable, the first newspaper accounts of foreign events to reach New York normally yielded a substantial profit to the importer, who could "scoop" his competitors.

16. *Truly Yours* (London: Samuel French Ltd., 1980), p. 1; and clipping, August 1955, Billy Rose Theatre Collection, New York Public Library.

17. *Truly Yours,* p. 1.

18. Ibid., p. 12.

19. "A Dramatic Center," *New York World,* 12 April 1878; *Wilson's Business Directory,* 1870-80; and *Trow's City Directory,* 1870-80.

20. According to Isadore Witmark in *The Story of the House of Witmark: From Ragtime to Swingtime* (New York: Lee Furman, Inc., 1939), his father, Marcus, had little to do with the routine management of the company. Naming the firm M. Witmark & Sons was an act of respect by his sons.

21. Newspaper clipping, n.d., Billy Rose Theatre Collection, New York Public Library.

22. Program for Robinson Hall, 1875, Harvard Theatre Collection.

23. Robert Grau, *The Businessman in the Amusement World* (New York: Broadway Publishing Company, 1910), p. 73.

24. Bernheim, *Business of the Theatre,* p. 41.

25. The booking of tours, however, continued to be effected on the sidewalks around the square until the advent of booking agencies in the 1880s.

26. Accepting a set fee or salary continued throughout the seventies. The practice of demanding a percentage of a star's gross receipts (a commission) was not adopted until the early eighties.

27. Bernheim, *Business of the Theatre,* p. 41.

28. Ibid., p. 42.

Chapter 9

1. James L. Ford, *Forty-Odd Years in the Literary Shop* (New York: E. P. Dutton & Company, 1921), p. 206.

2. The Broad Street restaurant was destroyed in a great fire of 1835 and was never rebuilt.

3. Lately Thomas, *Delmonico's: A Century of Splendor* (Boston: Houghton Mifflin Company, 1967), p. 83.

4. Ibid., p. 84.

5. Ibid., p. 83.

6. James Kotsilibas-Davis, *Great Times, Good Times* (Garden City, N.Y.: Doubleday & Co., Inc., 1977), p. 144.

7. *The Programme,* 20 April 1863; and newspaper clipping, "When Wallack's Opened," n.d., Harvard Theatre Collection.

8. Van Wyck, *Recollections,* p. 76.

9. E. Idell Zeisloft, ed., *The New Metropolis* (New York: D. Appleton and Company, 1899), p. 265.

10. Ford, *Forty-Odd Years,* pp. 211-12.

11. Zeisloft, *Metropolis,* p. 479.

12. Ibid., p. 266.

13. Ford, *Forty-Odd Years,* p. 208.

14. In D'Arcy's sentimental ballad, which begins, "Twas a balmy summer evening, and a goodly crowd was there./Which well-nigh filled Joe's barroom on the corner of the square," a pathetic vagabond narrates a story of a tragic love affair while sketching the face of his beloved on the barroom floor with a piece of chalk. Finishing the drawing, "he leaped and fell across the picture—dead." The ballad achieved fame during D'Arcy's lifetime and has been included in anthologies of American poetry.

15. Frank J. Prial, "Lüchow's, Symbol of the Good Old Days," *New York Times,* 24 March 1982.

16. Benjamin DeCasseres, "Lüchow's," *The American Mercury* (December 1931): 453; and Gerald Breitigam, "Down Where the Würtzburger Flows," *New York World-Telegram,* 7 April 1932.

17. "Down Where the Würtzburger Flows" was written by Vincent Bryan and Harry von Tilzer and first sung by Nora Bayes. The following year, von Tilzer wrote and published a sequel, titled "Under the Annheuser-Bush."

18. DeCasseres, "Lüchow's," p. 453.

19. Gemütlichkeit has been defined as a "state of mind, an easy-going disposition, a freedom from woe, comfortableness."

20. Michael and Ariane Batterberry, *On the Town in New York from 1776 to the Present* (New York: Charles Scribner's Sons, 1973), p. 133.

21. The first apartment house in America, the Rutherford-Stuyvesant Apartments at 142 E. 18th St., opened in 1869, but apartments (sometimes called French Flats) did not gain widespread acceptance until the 1880s.

22. Newspaper clipping, "The Rialto a Generation Ago," n.d., Bill Rose Theatre Collection, New York Public Library.

23. The "Amen Corner" located in a recess in the lobby of the Fifth Avenue Hotel was the unofficial meeting place for the leadership of the Republican Party, who routinely congregated there to formulate policy and plot strategy.

24. Kotsilibas-Davis, *Great Times,* p. 270.

25. Brown, *Valentine's Manual,* VIII, 158.

26. Moses King, *King's Handbook of New York City* (Boston: M. King, 1893), p. 234.

27. Thomas Lloyd, *Lloyd's Pocket Companion and Guide Through New York City for 1866-67* (New York: Torrey Brothers, Printers, 1866), p. 50; and Kenneth Holcomb Dunshee, *As You Pass By* (New York: Hastings House, 1952), p. 233.

28. Zeisloft, *Metropolis,* p. 298.

29. *Annals of the Lambs* (New York: Privately Printed, 1900), p. 3.

30. Gustave Kobbe, *Famous Actors and Their Homes* Boston: Little, Brown and Company, 1905), p. 194. If the Lambs had adhered strictly to their stated policy of admitting only 21 new members per year, this number should have been closer to 50 than 60. It is uncertain whether this number is incorrect or the club simply abandoned their initial admission quota.

31. The second famous actors' club, The Players, was founded the same year that the Lambs presented their first gambols. Created largely through the efforts of Edwin Booth, The Players maintained a clubhouse at 16 Gramercy Park (its present site) and from 1888, many prominent actors belonged to both clubs.

32. Louis Simon, *A History of the Actors' Fund of America* (New Theatre Arts Books, 1972), p. 44.

33. Ibid., p. 47.

34. Herbert Mitgang, "'100 Stars and More to Benefit Actors' Fund," *New York Times,* 6 January 1982; and Elinor Blau, "The Night is Filled with Stars for Actors' Fund Benefit," *New York Times,* 15 February 1982.

Chapter 10

1. Charles H. Gray, "The Old Rialto," newspaper clipping, n.d., Billy Rose Theatre Collection, New York Public Library.

2. Although the Irving Place was undeniably a first-class theatre, its years of prominence came too late for it to be considered among the important theatres of Union Square's Rialto period.

3. Odell, *Annals,* XV, 382.

4. Between 1894 and 1896, the only movies available to the public were of the "peep show" variety; but during this period, a secret race was taking place to determine which of several projectors (the Edison-Armat vitascope, the Lumière cinematograph, the American biograph, and the Latham pantoptikon) would be the first to be shown publicly. This race also involved vaudeville impresarios, B. F. Keith, Oscar Hammerstein, and the partnership of John Koster and Adam Bial. The race was won on 23 April 1896 when Koster and Bial introduced the Edison-Armat machine. Two months later, Keith introduced the Lumière cinematograph at the Union Square Theatre and on 12 October 1896, less than six months after the vitascope was first exhibited, Oscar Hammerstein sponsored the world premiere of the American biograph at the Olympia Music Hall.

5. While formerly called automatic vaudeville, the arcade films were more commonly known as "penny dreadfuls."

6. Although there had been attempts to show projected movies in converted storefronts as early as 1902 (most notably Thomas Tally's "Electric Theatre" in Los Angeles), all efforts prior to Davis and Harris's nickelodeon in McKeesport were shortlived. As a result, film historians generally credit Davis and Harris with establishing the first successful theatre devoted solely to showing projected movies.

7. Joseph H. North, *The Early Development of the Motion Picture* (New York: Arno Press, 1973), pp. 238-39.

8. Dulles, *America Learns to Play,* p. 289.

9. The famous film company, known simply as Biograph in its later days, took its original title, the K.M.C.D. Syndicate, from the initials of its founders' last names. The name of the firm was subsequently changed to the American Mutoscope Company when the mutoscope was developed in the fall of 1895 and then to the American Mutoscope and Biograph Company with the addition of the American biograph in 1896.

10. According to film historian, Terry Ramsaye, this was the first liaison between Wall Street, big business, and the movie industry.

11. Ironically, one of Biograph's early films documented the demolition of the Star Theatre.

12. Robert M. Henderson, *D. W. Griffith: His Life and Work* (New York: Oxford University Press, 1972), pp. 15-34.

13. Terry Ramsaye, *A Million and One Nights* (New York: Simon and Schuster, 1926), p. 452.

14. Grau, *Businessman in the Amusement World,* pp. 131-32.

15. Fox evidently was skeptical about the City's future as a legitimate house from the outset. His only instruction to Thomas Lamb was to include a permanent projection booth in the plans for the theatre.

16. *New York Times,* 19 April 1910.

17. The Motion Picture Patents Company, formed in 1908, was composed of the most important producing firms in the film industry. Like the U.B.O. and the Theatrical Syndicate, the film trust attempted to monopolize an industry by controlling distribution and exhibition of its particular form of entertainment.

18. Ben M. Hall, *The Golden Age of the Movie Palace* (New York: Clarkson N. Potter, Inc., Publisher, 1961), pp. 32-40.

19. Robert Grau, "Old New York Theatres," *New York Dramatic Mirror,* 7 July 1915.

Bibliography

Books

Alden, Cynthia M. Westover. *Manhattan, Historic and Artistic.* New York: The Morse Company, 1897.

Anderson, John. *The American Theatre: An Interpretive History.* New York: The Dial Press, 1938.

Annals of The Lambs. New York: Privately printed, 1900.

Appelbaum, Stanley, ed. *The New York Stage; Famous Productions in Photographs.* New York: Dover Publications, Inc., 1976.

Appleton's Dictionary of New York City. New York: A. Appleton & Co., 1884.

Atkinson, Brooks. *Broadway.* New York: Macmillan Publishing Co., Inc., 1974.

Baker, H. Barton. *History of the London Stage.* New York: Benjamin Blom, 1904.

Barth, Gunther. *City People: The Rise of Modern City Culture in Nineteenth-Century America.* New York: Oxford University Press, 1980.

Barton, George De Forest. "Union Square" in *Valentine's Manual of Old New York.* Vol. 7. 1922, pp. 194-209.

Bassham, Ben L. *The Theatrical Photographs of Napoleon Sarony.* Kent, Ohio: The Kent State University Press, 1978.

Batterberry, Michael and Ariane. *On the Town in New York from 1776 to the Present.* New York: Charles Scribner's Sons, 1973.

Belden, E. Porter. *New York: Past, Present and Future.* New York: Geo. P. Putnam, 1849.

Bernheim, Alfred L. *The Business of the Theatre: An Economic History of the American Theatre, 1750-1932.* New York: Benjamin Blom, 1932.

Black, Mary. *Old New York in Early Photographs.* New York: Dover Publications, Inc., 1973.

Blum, Daniel. *A Pictorial History of the American Theatre: 1860-1976.* 4th ed. Revised by John Willis. New York: Crown Publishers, Inc., 1977.

Bowman, Ned A. "Held Up to Yankee Nature," in *The American Theatre: A Sum of its Parts.* London: Samuel French, Inc., 1971, pp. 199-222.

Bradstreet's Business Directory of New York City for 1876. New York: Bradstreet and Wilcox, 1876.

Brockett, Oscar G. *History of the Theatre.* 3rd ed. Boston: Allyn and Bacon, Inc., 1977.

Brown, Henry Collins. *Brownstone Fronts and Saratoga Trunks.* New York: E. P. Dutton & Co., Inc., 1935.

‗‗‗‗‗. *Delmonico's.* New York: Valentine's Manual, 1928.

‗‗‗‗‗. *Fifth Avenue Old and New.* New York: Wynkoup Hallenbeck Crawford Co., 1924.

‗‗‗‗‗, ed. *Valentine's Manual of Old New York.* 12 vols. New York: Various Publishers, 1916-1928

‗‗‗‗‗. *Walks and Tours Around New York.* New York: Valentine's Manual Inc., 1924.

Brown, T. Allston. *A History of the New York Stage: From the First Performance in 1732 to 1901.* 3 vols. New York: Benjamin Blom, 1963. Originally published 1903.

Browne, Junius Henri. *The Great Metropolis: A Mirror of New York.* Hartford: American Publishing Company, 1869.

Burdick, Jacques. *Theater.* New York: Newsweek Books, 1974.

Cahn, Julius. *Julius Cahn's Official Theatrical Guide.* New York: Publication Office, Empire Theatre Building, 1899-1905.

Carroll, David. *The Matinee Idols.* New York: Arbor House, 1972.

Carroll's New York City Directory. New York: Carroll & Company, 1859.

Chancellor, E. Beresford. *The Pleasure Haunts of London.* London: Constable & Company Ltd., 1925.

Cheney, Sheldon. *The Theatre: Three Thousand Years of Drama, Acting and Stagecraft.* New York: David McKay Company, Inc., 1929.

Churchill, Allen. *The Great White Way.* New York: E. P. Dutton & Co., Inc., 1962.

_____. *The Theatrical Twenties.* New York: McGraw-Hill Book Company, 1975.

_____. *The Upper Crust.* Englewood Cliffs, N.J.: Prentice-Hall, Inc., 1970.

The Citizen and Strangers' Guide for the City of New York and its Vicinity. New York: Charles Spaulding & Co., Publishers, 1853.

The City of New York: A Complete Guide. New York: Taintor Brothers, 1870.

Coad, Oral Sumner, and Mims, Edwin Jr. *The American Stage.* New Haven: Yale University Press, 1929.

Csida, Joseph, and Csida, June Bundy. *American Entertainment: A Unique History of Popular Show Business.* New York: A Billboard Book, 1978.

Delgado, Alan. *Victorian Entertainment.* New York: American Heritage Press, 1971.

Diagrams of Leading Theatres, Opera Houses, Concert Halls, and Athletic Fields. New York: The City News Publishing Co., 1922.

Dimeglio, John E. *Vaudeville U.S.A.* Bowling Green, Ohio: Bowling Green University Popular Press, 1973.

Dimmick, Ruth Crosby. *Our Theatres To-day and Yesterday.* New York: The H. K. Fly Company, Publishers, 1913.

Disternell, John. *New York As It Was and As It Is.* New York: n.p., 1876.

Dulles, Foster Rhea. *America Learns to Play: A History of Popular Recreation.* New York: D. Appleton-Century Company, 1940.

Dunshee, Kenneth Holcomb. *As You Pass By.* New York: Hastings House, 1952.

Durant, John, and Durant, Alice. *Pictorial History of the American Circus.* New York: A. S. Barnes and Company, 1957.

Durso, Joseph. *Madison Square Garden: 100 Years of History.* New York: Simon and Schuster, 1979.

Eaton, Walter Prichard. *The American Theatre of To-day.* Boston: Small, Maynard and Company, 1908.

Eustis, Morton, *B'way, Inc: The Theatre as a Business.* New York: Benjamin Blom, Inc., 1934.

Everson, William K. *American Silent Film.* New York: Oxford University Press, 1978.

Fiske, Harrison Grey, ed. *The New York Mirror Annual and Directory of the Theatrical Profession for 1888.* New York: New York Mirror, 1888.

Footner, Hulbert. *New York, City of Cities.* London: J. B. Lippincott Company, 1937.

Ford, James L. *Forty-Odd Years in the Literary Shop.* New York: E. P. Dutton & Company, 1921.

Freedley, George, and Reeves, John A. *A History of the Theatre.* New York: Crown Publishers, Inc., 1955.

Gilbert, Douglas. *American Vaudeville: Its Life and Times.* New York: Dover Publications, Inc., 1940.

Girard, Stephen. *The Merchants' Sketch Book.* New York: n.p., 1844.

Grafton, John. *New York in the Nineteenth Century.* New York: Dover Publications, Inc., 1977.

Grau, Robert. *The Business Man in the Amusement World.* New York: Broadway Publishing Company, 1910.

_____. *The Theatre of Science.* reissued; New York: Benjamin Blom, 1969.

Griffith, Mrs. D. W. *When the Movies Were Young.* New York: Benjamin Blom, 1925.

Grout, Donald Jay. *A Short History of Opera.* New York: Columbia University Press, 1947.

Guide of the City of New York. New York: H. J. Kleefish, 1859.

Hall, Ben M. *The Golden Age of the Movie Palace.* New York: Clarkson N. Potter, Inc., Publisher, 1961.

Harris, Charles Townsend. *Memories of Manhattan in the Sixties and Seventies.* New York: The Derrydale Press, 1928.

Hemstreet, Charles. *The Broadway of Yesterday.* New York: Cadwallader, 1905.

_____. *Nooks and Corners of Old New York.* New York: Charles Scribner's Sons, 1899.

Henderson, Mary C. *The City and the Theatre.* Clifton, N.J.: James T. White & Company, 1973.

Henderson, Robert M. *D. W. Griffith: His Life and Work.* New York: Oxford University Press, 1972.

Hewitt, Barnard. *Theatre U.S.A.* New York: McGraw-Hill Book Company, Inc., 1959.

Hornblow, Arthur. *A History of the Theatre in America.* 2 vols. New York: Benjamin Blom, 1965. Originally published 1919.

Hornung, Clarence P. *The Way it Was: New York, 1850-1890.* New York: Schocken Books, 1977.

Hotel Guests' Guide for the City of New York. n.p. 1871.

Hughes, Glenn. *A History of the American Theatre.* New York: Samuel French, 1951.

Hungerford, Edward. *Pathway of Empire.* New York: Robert M. McBride & Company, 1935.

Illustrated New York: The Metropolis of To-Day. New York: International Publishing Co., 1888.

Ireland, Joseph N. *Records of the New York Stage from 1750 to 1960.* 2 vols. New York: Burt Franklin, 1968.

James, Theodore. *Fifth Avenue.* New York: Walker, 1971.

Janvier, Thomas A. *In Old New York.* New York: Garrett Press, 1968.

Jefferson, Joseph. *The Autobiography of Joseph Jefferson.* Ed. Alan S. Downer. Cambridge: The Belknap Press of Harvard University Press, 1964.

Jennings, John J. *Theatrical and Circus Life, or, Secrets of the Stage, Greenroom and Sawdust Arena.* St. Louis: M. S. Barnett, 1882.

Kelley, Frank Bergan. *Historical Guide to the City of New York.* New York: Frederick A. Stokes Company, 1909.

Kielty, Bernardine. *The Sidewalks of New York.* New York: Little Leather Library Corporation, 1923.

King, Moses. *King's Handbook of New York City.* Boston: M. King, 1893.

_____. *New York: The American Cosmopolis.* Boston: Moses King, 1894.

Klein, Alexander. *The Empire City.* New York: Rinehart & Company, Inc., 1955.

Kobbe, Gustav. *Famous Actors and their Homes.* Boston: Little, Brown and Company, 1905.

Koch, Roby. *Louis C. Tiffany, Rebel in Glass.* New York: Crown Publishers, Inc., 1966.

Kotsilibas-Davis, James. *Great Times, Good Times.* Garden City, N.Y.: Doubleday & Co., Inc., 1977.

Kouwenhoven, John A. *The Columbia Historical Portrait of New York:* New York: Harper & Row, Publishers, 1953.

Krehbiel, Henry Edward. *Chapters of Opera.* New York: Henry Holt and Company, 1908.

Lamb, Mrs. Martha J., and Harrison, Mrs. Burton. *History of the City of New York.* 3 vols. New York: A. S. Barnes and Company, 1877.

The Lambs. New York: Wm. C. Martin Printing House, 1897.

Lansing's Pictorial Diagrams of the Leading Opera Houses, Theatres, etc. In the United States. Boston: Lansing & Co. Publishers, 1880.

Laurie, Joe Jr. *Vaudeville: From the Honky-Tonks to the Palace.* Port Washington, N.Y.: Kennikat Press, 1953.

Leavitt, Michael. *Fifty Years in Theatrical Management.* New York: Broadway Publishing Co., 1912.

LeGallienne, Eva. *At 33.* New York: Longmans, Green & Co., 1940.

_____. *With a Quiet Heart.* New York: Viking Press, 1953.

Leuchs, Fritz A. H. *The Early German Theatre in New York.* New York: Columbia University Press, 1928.

Lightfoot, Frederick S., ed. *Nineteenth-Century New York in Rare Photographic Views.* New York: Dover Publications, Inc., 1981.

Lloyd, Thomas. *Lloyd's Pocket Companion and Guide Through New York City for 1866-67.* New York: Torrey Brothers, Printers, 1866.

Lockwood, Charles. *Manhattan Moves Uptown.* Boston: Houghton Mifflin Company, 1976.

Lyman, Susan. *100 New York Years.* n.p., 1948.

McCabe, James D. *Lights and Shadows of New York Life.* Philadelphia: National Publishing Co., 1872. Facsimile Edition: New York: Farrar, Straus and Giroux, 1970.

Macoy, Robert. *The Centennial Guide to New York and its Environs.* New York: Robert Macoy, 1876; reprint ed., New York: Nathan Cohen Books, 1975.

Magriel, Paul. *Chronicles of the American Dance.* New York: DaCapo Press, 1948.

Mander, Raymond, and Mitchenson, Joe. *British Music Hall.* London: London House and Maxwell, 1965.

_____. *The Theatres of London.* London: Rupert Hart-Davis, 1961.

Mantzius, Karl. *A History of Theatrical Art.* Trans. Louise von Cossel. 6 vols. New York: Peter Smith, 1937.

Marcuse, Maxwell F. *This Was New York.* New York: LIM Press, 1969.

Martin, Edward Winslow. *Secrets of the Great City.* Philadelphia: Jones, Brothers & Co., 1868.

Mates, Julian. *The American Musical Stage Before 1800.* New Brunswick, N.J.: Rutgers University Press, 1962.

Matlaw, Myron, ed. *American Popular Entertainment: Papers and Proceedings of the Conference on the History of American Popular Entertainment.* Westport, CT: Greenwood Press, 1977.

Mayer, Grace. *Once Upon a City.* New York: Macmillan Company, 1958.

Miller's New York As It Is. New York: James Miller, 1860.

Mines, John Flavel. *A Tour Around New York and My Summer Acre being the Recreations of Mr. Felix Oldboy.* New York: Harper & Brothers, 1892.

Mitchell, Lucy Sprague, and Lambert, Clara. *Manhattan Now and Long Ago.* New York: The Macmillan Company, 1934.

Moody, Richard. *Ned Harrigan: From Corlear's Hook to Herald Square.* Chicago: Nelson-Hall, 1980.

Moore, Thomas Gale. *The Economics of the American Theater.* Durham, N.C.: Duke University Press, 1968.

Morehouse, Ward. *Matinee Tomorrow.* New York: McGraw-Hill Book Company, Inc., 1949.

Morris, Lloyd. *Incredible New York: High Life and Low Life of the Last Hundred Years.* New York: Random House, 1951.

Nevins, Allan, and Thomas, Milton Halsey, eds. *The Diary of George Templeton Strong.* 4 vols. New York: The Macmillan Company, 1952.

New York, 1895. New York: A. F. Parsons Publishing Co., 1895.

New York City Directory. New York: Chas. R. Rode, 1850-95.

New York City Guide. New York: Random House, 1939.

New York City Guide. New York: Octagon Books, 1870.

New York Illustrated. New York: D. Appleton & Co., 1869.

North, Joseph H. *The Early Development of the Motion Picture.* New York: Arno Press, 1973.

Odell, George C. D. *Annals of the New York Stage.* 15 vols. New York: Columbia University Press, 1927-1941.

Osgood, Frances S. *The Cries of New York.* New York: John Doggett, Jr., 1846.

Pelletreau, William S. *Early New York Houses.* New York: Francis P. Harper, Publisher, 1900.

Peterson, A. Everett. *Landmarks of New York.* New York: The City History Club of New York, 1923.

Poggi, Jack. *Theater in America: The Impact of Economic Forces, 1870-1967.* Ithaca, N.Y.: Cornell University Press, 1966.

Powers, James T. *Twinkle Little Star.* New York: G. P. Putnam's Sons, 1939.

Ramsaye, Terry. *A Million and One Nights.* New York: Simon and Schuster, 1926.

The Real Estate Record Association, *Real Estate, Building and Architecture in New York City During the Last Quarter of a Century.* New York: Record and Guide, 1898.

Richmond, Rev. J. F. *New York and its Institutions.* New York: E. B. Treat, 1871.

Rider, Fremont. *Rider's New York City: A Guidebook for Travellers.* 2nd ed. New York: The Macmillan Company, 1924.

Rogers, Cleveland, and Rankin, Rebecca B. *New York: The World's Capital City.* New York: Harper & Brothers, 1948.

Roth, Hy, and Cromie, Robert. *The Little People.* New York: Everest House, 1980.

Sanders, Ronald. *The Lower East Side.* New York: Dover Publications, Inc., 1979.

Seilhamer, George O. *History of the American Theatre.* 3 vols. New York: Benjamin Blom, 1968.

Simon, Kate. *Fifth Avenue: A Very Social History.* New York: Harcourt Brace Jovanovich, 1979.

Simon, Louis M. *A History of the Actors' Fund of America.* New York: Theatre Arts Books, 1972.

Sobel, Bernard. *A Pictorial History of Vaudeville.* New York: Citadel Press, 1961.

Steinberg, Mollie B. *The History of the Fourteenth Street Theatre.* New York: The Dial Press, 1931.

Still, Bayrd. *Mirror for Gotham.* New York: New York University Press, 1956.

Stoddard, J. H. *Recollections of a Player.* New York: The Century Co., 1902.

Stokes, I. N. Phelps. *The Iconography of Manhattan Island: 1498-1909.* 6 vols. New York: Robert H. Dodd, 1916.

_____. *New York Past and Present: Its History and Landmarks 1524-1939.* n.p., 1939.

Stone, Henry Dickenson. *Personal Recollections of the Drama.* New York: Benjamin Blom, 1873. Republished 1969.

The Stranger's Guide Around New York and its Vicinity, n.p. 1853.

Stratman, Carl J. *American Theatrical Periodicals, 1798-1967: A Bibliographical Guide.* Durham, N.C.: Duke University Press, 1970.

Taubman, Howard. *The Making of the American Theatre.* New York: Coward McCann, Inc., 1965.

Thomas, Lately. *Delmonico's: A Century of Splendor.* Boston: Houghton Mifflin Company, 1967.

Tidworth, Simon. *Theatres: An Architectural and Cultural History.* New York: Praeger Publishers, 1973.

Toll, Robert C. *Blacking Up.* London: Oxford University Press, 1974.

_____. *On with the Show.* New York: Oxford University Press, 1976.

Towse, John Rankin. *Sixty Years of the Theater.* New York: Funk & Wagnalls Company, 1916.

Trow's New York City Directory. New York: The Trow City Directory Company, 1863-95.

Truly Yours. London: Samuel French Ltd., 1980.

Tyson, Henry H. *Diagrams of New York and Brooklyn Theatres.* New York: Willis McDonald Co., Printers, 1887.

Van Wyck, Frederick. *Recollections of an Old New Yorker.* New York: Liveright Inc., Publishers, 1932.

Vardac, A. Nicholas. *Stage to Screen.* Cambridge: Harvard University Press, 1949.

Wallack, Lester. *Memories of Fifty Years.* New York: Charles Scribner's Sons, 1889.

Watson, Edward B. *New York Then and Now.* New York: Dover Publications, Inc., 1976.

Weitenkampf, Frank. *Manhattan Kaleidoscope.* New York: Charles Scribner's Sons, 1947.

Wharton, Edith. "The Age of Innocence," in *The Edith Wharton Omnibus.* New York: Charles Scribner's Sons, 1978.

Whitman, Walt. *New York Dissected.* New York: Rufus Rockwell Wilson, Inc., 1936.

Wilmeth, Don B. *The Language of American Popular Entertainment.* Westport, CT: Greenwood Press, 1981.

Wilson's Business Directory of New York City. New York: The Trow City Directory Company, 1870-95.

Wilson, Garff B. *Three Hundred Years of American Drama and Theatre.* Englewood Cliffs, N.J.: Prentice-Hall, Inc., 1973.

Wilson, Rufus Rockwell. *New York: Old and New.* 2 vols. Philadelphia: J. B. Lippincott Company, 1902.

Witmark, Isadore, and Goldberg, Isaac. *The Story of the House of Witmark: From Ragtime to Swingtime.* New York: Lee Furman, Inc., 1939.

Young, William C. *Documents of American Theatre History.* 2 vols. Chicago: American Library Association, 1973.

Zeidman, Irving. *The American Burlesque Show.* New York: Hawthorn Books, Inc., 1967.

Zeisloft, E. Idell, ed. *The New Metropolis*. New York: D. Appleton and Company, 1899.

Zellers, Parker. *Tony Pastor. Dean of the Vaudeville Stage*. Ypsilanti, Mich.: Eastern Michigan University Press, 1971.

Articles in Periodicals and Newspapers

"The Academy of Music." *Evening Post*, 2 February 1887.

"The Academy of Music." *New York Dramatic Mirror*, 18 June 1910.

"Academy of Music Closed Forever." *New York Times*, 18 May 1926.

"Academy Passes." *New York Tribune*, 5 June 1910.

"Agnes Ethel Dead." *New York Sun*, 27 May 1903.

"A. M. Palmer Dies From Apoplexy." *New York Herald*, 8 March 1905.

A. M. Palmer Obituary. *The Evening Sun*, 8 March 1905.

"Another Huber Enterprise." *New York Recorder*, 28 June 1895.

"At Huber's." *New York Recorder-Sun*, 28 June 1895.

"At the Theatres." *New York Dramatic Mirror*, 24 October 1885.

"At the Theatres." *New York Dramatic Mirror*, 27 October 1888.

Atkinson, J. Brooks. "Art in Fourteenth Street." *Civic Repertory Magazine* 1 (November 1930): 4.

Austin, W. W. "The American Stage a Generation Ago." *Theatre Magazine* 14 (August 1911): 64-70

Barry, Ed. "Tony Pastor—A Strictly Personal Showman." *Variety*, 4 January 1956.

Blau, Elinor. "The Night is Filled with Stars for Actors' Fund Benefit Gala." *New York Times*, 15 February 1982.

"Boston Manager in New York." *Boston Herald*, 18 September 1893.

Breitigam, Gerald B. "A Songbirds' Nest in Union Square." *New York World-Telegram*, 6 April 1932.

————. "Down Where the Würtzburger Flowed." *New York World-Telegram*, 7 April 1932.

Brown, T. Allston. Series of articles on New York Theatres, *New York Clipper*, 1893.

George B. Bunnell Obituary. *New York Clipper*, 13 May 1911.

"A City Theatre in Ashes." *New York World*. 29 February 1888.

"Curtain to Ring Down on Famous Theatre." *New York World*, 20 April 1901.

"Dazian's." *The New Yorker*, 8 October 1932, p. 13.

DeCasseres, Benjamin. "Lüchow's." *The American Mercury*, December 1931, pp. 447-54.

"Delmonico's Famous Line." *New York Sun*, 29 September 1901.

Devorkin, Joseph. "The Morton House." *The Villager*, 31 July 1969.

"A Dramatic Center." *New York World*, 12 April 1878, p. 5.

Drieblatt, Martha. "Exit Civic Repertory Theatre: Aged 72." *New York Herald Tribune*, 8 May 1938.

Dunning, Jennifer. "A Diamond Jim Brady Eating-Palace Tour." *New York Times*, 26 March 1982.

————. "A Singing Tour of the Gay 90's Tin Pan Alley." *New York Times*, 16 July 1982.

"The End of Wallack's Theatre." *Boston Evening Transcript*, 1 May 1915.

"Fitting Dramatic Survival: The Stock Companies of the Past and of the Present." *Harper's Weekly*, 22 February 1902.

Ford, James L. "Commercialism in the Theatre." *Scribner's Magazine*, March 1917, pp. 284-86.

————. "Movies Where our Rural Drama was Born." *The Evening Post Magazine*, 3 April 1920, pp. 4, 5.

————. "The Shifting Night Life of New York." *Vanity Fair*, February 1917, pp. 37, 96.

Grau, Robert. "New York Theatres Some Forty Odd Years Ago." *The American Architect*, 31 December 1913, pp. 280-81.

————. "Old New York Theatres." *New York Dramatic Mirror*, 7 July 1915.

Gray, Barry. "The Good Old Days of the Dime Museum." *Billboard*, 8 December 1928, pp. 98-99.

Henderson, W. J. "Some New York Theatres." *The Magazine of Art*, 1886.

"How the Curtain Fell Forever on the Fine Old Star," *The Evening Sun*, 22 April 1901.

"Huber's Museum in the Discard." *New York Telegraph*, 17 July 1910.

"Keith's Union Square Theatre." *New York Recorder-Sun,* 28 July 1895.

Krehbiel, H. E. "Recollections and Records of a Quarter Century of Grand Opera." *New York Tribune,* 5 July 1908.

LaShelle, K. "Theatrical Advance Agent." *Cosmopolitan,* January 1900, pp. 325-30.

Lightfoot, Helen V. "Past Glories of the Academy of Music." *Theatre Magazine* 9 (May 1909): 146, 148, 150.

MacGowan, Kenneth. "The Crisis on Broadway." *Harper's Magazine,* December 1928.

McNamara, Brooks. "A Congress of Wonders": The Rise and Fall of the Dime Museum." *Emerson Society Quarterly* 20 (3rd Quarter 1974): 216-32.

Matlaw, Myron. "Pastor and his Flock." *Theatre Arts,* August 1958, pp. 20-21.

_____. Review of *Tony Pastor: Dean of the Vaudeville Stage* by Parker Zellers. *Educational Theatre Journal* 24 (October 1972): 336-37.

Mitgang, Herbert. "'100 Stars and More to Benefit Actors' Fund." *New York Times,* 6 January 1982.

"Mystery Skeleton of Union Square." *New York Journal-American,* 14 June 1964.

"New York's Changing Scene." *Sunday News,* 18 March 1956.

"New York's Changing Scene." *Sunday News,* 15 February 1959.

"New York Daguerreotyped." *Putnam's Monthly,* Vol. I, no. 2, February 1853; vol. I, no. 4, April 1853; vol. III, no. 15, March 1854.

Odom, Leigh George. "The Black Crook at Niblo's Garden." *The Drama Review* 26 (Spring 1982): 21-40.

"Old 14th Street Theatre to Go." *New York Sun,* 19 October 1936.

Ormsbee, Helen. "The Union Square Theatre Takes a Very Final Curtain." *New York Herald-Tribune,* 6 September 1936.

Overmyer, Grace. "Seventy Years in New York Concert Halls." *New York Tribune,* 16 March 1924, pp. 12-13.

"The Passing of the Star Theatre." *The Evening Sun,* 23 December 1899.

"Passing of Theatrical Landmark to Make Way for Business." *New York Herald,* 12 March 1899.

"Pastor in Charge Again." *Variety,* 18 July 1908.

"Pastor Looking for New Theatre." *New York Telegraph,* 28 June 1908.

Patterson, Ada. "A Chat with Old Josh Whitcomb." *Theatre Magazine* 8 (July 1908): 192-94.

Prial, Frank J. "Luchow's, Symbol of the Good Old Days." *New York Times,* 24 March 1982.

Rankin, Mrs. McKee. "Behind the Scenes with the Two Orphans." *Theatre Magazine* 11 (May 1910): 157-60.

Reamer, Lawrence. "The Drama." *Harper's Weekly,* 4 May 1901.

Reardon, William R. "The American Drama and Theatre in the Nineteenth Century: A Retreat from Meaning." *Emerson Society Quarterly* 20 (3rd Quarter 1974): 170-77.

_____, and Bristow, Eugene K. "The American Theatre, 1864-1870: An Economic Portrait." *Speech Monographs* 33 (November 1966): 438-43.

"Recollections of the Old Star which is Soon to be Torn Down." *The Mail and Express,* 6 April 1901.

Reed, Henry Hope. "The Old Rialto." *New York Herald Tribune,* 19 August 1962, p. 2.

Ripley, John W. "Those Were the Good Old Nickelodeon Days." *Smithsonian* 12 (March 1982): 76-83.

Napoleon Sarony Obituary. *New York Dramatic Mirror,* 21 November 1896.

"The Second Wallack's." *New York Tribune,* 16 June 1899.

Shane, Ted. "Broadway's Country Store." *Collier's,* 13 November 1948, pp. 36, 38.

"Sheridan Shook Dies on his Farm." *New York Herald,* 29 April 1899.

Smith, Milo L. "The Klaw-Erlanger Bogyman Myth." *Players* 44 (Dec.-Jan. 1969): 70-75.

Squire, Tom. "Manhattan Odyssey." *Theatre Arts Monthly* 23 (August 1939): 585-96.

St. John, Molyneaux. "New York Theatres." *Broadway,* September 1867-August 1868, pp. 473-79.

"Star Theatre Goes; Old Patrons Sad." *New York Journal,* 3 December 1899.

Steinberg, Mollie B. "History of the Fourteenth Street Theatre." *Civic Repertory Magazine* 1, no. 2 (November 1930): 4; 1, no. 4 (December 1930): 8.

"Street Changes: Concentration of Retail Trade at Union Square." *New York Times*, 21 November 1867.

"Successful Opera at the Fourteenth Street Theatre." *New York Sun*, 30 April 1938.

Thomas, Irwin. "Tony Pastor's Theatre to Pass with Going of Old Tammany." *The Evening World*, 28 April 1926.

"Tony Pastor Celebrates His 43rd Anniversary." *Variety*, 28 March 1908, p. 10.

"Tony Pastor Looking for a New Theatre." *New York Telegraph*, 28 June 1908.

"Tournament of the Billiard Champions." *New York Times*, 3 September 1866.

"Twas Merry Christmas, Mr. Brown on Union Square 80 Years Ago." *Gramercy Graphic*, December 1959, p. 10.

"The Union Square of Old." *New York Herald*, 28 January 1923.

"Union Square Turns the Century Mark." *Gas Logic*, May 1932.

"Vaudevillists: Their Acts and Where to Find Them." *The Trouper*, July 1905.

Weed, Raphael A. "The New York Stage in Photography." *The New York Historical Quarterly Bulletin* XIV (April 1930-January 1931): 47-67.

"Welcome New City Theatre." *New York Times*, 19 April 1910.

"What's in a Name? Union Square." *New York Evening Sun*, 18 November 1919.

Wilstach, Paul. "Richard Mansfield—His Beginnings and Apprenticeship." *Scribner's Magazine*, September 1908, pp. 66-76.

"Wiped Out by Fire. The Union Square a Smoldering Wreck." *New York Star*, 29 February 1888.

Unpublished Materials

Chandler, Thelma. Unpublished paper, n.d. Museum of the City of New York.

Cronin, David E. *Union Square*. Unpublished manuscript. 1922. New York Historical Society.

Garrett, Thomas M. "A History of Pleasure Gardens in New York City, 1700-1865." Ph.D. Dissertation, New York University, 1978.

Jones, Cecil Derwent, Jr. "The Policies and Practices of Wallack's Theatre." Ph.D. Dissertation, University of Illinois, 1959.

Rambusch, Catha Grace. "Museums and Other Collections in New York City, 1790-1870." M. A. Thesis, New York University, 1965.

Ryan, Pat M. Jr. "A. M. Palmer, Producer: A Study of Management, Dramaturgy, and Stagecraft in the American Theatre, 1872-96." Ph.D. Dissertation, Yale University, 1959.

Simpson, Sarah H. J. "New York in 1868." Unpublished manuscript. n.d. New York Historical Society.

Weitenkampf, Frank. "Union Square in Change." Unpublished paper in Union Square file, New York Public Library.

Newspapers

The Amusement Gazette
Frank Leslie's Illustrated Newspaper
Harper's Weekly
The *New York Clipper*
The *New York Dramatic Mirror*
The *New York Herald*
The *New York Sun*
The *New York Times*
The *New York Tribune*
The Spirit of the Times

Miscellaneous

Clippings, programs, souvenir booklets, playbills, pictures, posters, and correspondence in the Billy Rose Theatre Collection, the New York Public Library; the Theatre Collection, the Museum of the City of New York; the Harvard Theatre Collection; the Princeton Theatre Collection; the Walter Hampden-Edwin Booth Theatre Collection, The Players; the Local History and Genealogy Room, the New York Public Library; and the Print Room and the Research Library, the New York Historical Society.

Index